RUSSIAN HARVEST

KEN MURPHY

Woman's Missionary Union

Birmingham, Alabama

Woman's Missionary Union
P. O. Box 830010
Birmingham, AL 35283-0010

For more information, visit our Web site at www.wmu.com or call 1-800-968-7301.

Dewey Decimal Classification: 266.647
Subject Headings: MISSIONS—RUSSIA
BAPTISTS—KENTUCKY
BAPTISTS—RUSSIA
RUSSIA—RELIGION

Design by Janell E. Young

Photos courtesy of Ken Murphy

ISBN: 1-56309-694-3
W994122•0999•5M1

For Robbie

CONTENTS

1

A LONG WAY FROM HOME

White! As far as I could see, everything was white. The big Delta jet emerged from a low cloud ceiling in preparation for our landing in Moscow; and for the first time in my life, I looked out onto the vast Russian landscape. The deep January snow blanketed everything, the bleakness intensified by the heavily overcast sky.

As the plane touched down, I tried to distinguish details in the unfamiliar view outside my window. The runway appeared freshly scraped, but a layer of snow remained. Scattered buildings and airplanes interrupted the whiteness, but they did little to dispel the pervasive gloom. In the gathering dusk of the early Moscow evening, everything looked dismal and cold. Well, it could be worse, I thought. At least I was in a warm aircraft, and soon I would deplane through a jetway and enter the terminal.

The first of many surprises came as the plane pulled to a stop at a remote location on the snow-covered tarmac. I could see two other planes from my window. The snow covering them indicated that they had been there for some time. Was something wrong? Were we being denied permission to enter Russia? It was easy to imagine such things. This was, after all, *Russia*. A couple of years of "lessening tensions" could not dismiss a lifetime of stories about Communist repression and cold-war hostilities.

After a few minutes' wait, the pilot instructed us to exit the plane by a stairway being wheeled into place. He explained that a bus would drive us to the terminal. Taking my place in the line of passengers, I walked down the steps into the cold air. Two guards holding machine guns directed us toward the bus parked behind the plane. Other machine-gun-toting guards waited by the bus. I recalled Dorothy's words in *The Wizard of Oz:* "Toto, I have a feeling we're not in Kansas anymore."

Or Kentucky! I had never felt so far from home. It had been a long journey, in many ways. And the road was not well traveled. Where did it all begin?

In 1983, Bill Marshall left what was then the Foreign Mission Board (now International Mission Board; IMB) of the Southern Baptist Convention to become executive secretary-treasurer of the Kentucky Baptist Convention. With him he brought a passion and vision for doing missions in a bold new way: teams of short-term volunteers partnering with career missionaries for strategic projects on their missions fields. Kentucky Baptists soon recognized this as an effective way of fulfilling the Great Commission.

Kentucky Baptists launched such a 3-year partnership with the east African nation of Kenya in 1985. Kenyan nationals and the volunteer missions team were both well positioned for this partnership, and the results were phenomenal. The number of Kenyan Baptist churches grew by over 1,000—an average of 1 per day—thanks to the efforts of the Kenyans and the 779 Kentucky Baptists who participated. By the time this partnership ended in 1987, the number of Kenyan Baptist churches had doubled. Since then, the number has doubled again.

The Brazilian state of Espirito Santo (Holy Spirit in English) became Kentucky Baptists' next partner, a relationship which lasted from 1989 through 1993. The name characterizes what Kentucky volunteers and their Brazilian partners experienced. Nothing else could account for the success the 850 Kentucky Baptists witnessed, with the number of new Christian converts averaging five for each volunteer.

As Kentucky Baptist volunteers labored faithfully in these two missions fields, few, if any, could see across the tapestry of world events and imagine the unique opportunity God was weaving.

The Iron Curtain was falling in Russia, and the greatest challenge yet in partnership missions emerged on the horizon.

Mikhail Gorbachev became general secretary of the Communist Party in 1985, and words like *glasnost* (openness) and *perestroika* (restructuring) began to define a new Russia. By the end of that decade, Communism had fallen in Russia, and the country was open to the outside world. With these changes came an unprecedented religious freedom. In a country where atheism had been the official religion for most of the century, Christians could now preach and teach the gospel message without limits.

While the Russian Orthodox Church had endured its share of persecution and restrictions, it still maintained a kind of state church status in the country. Now, at least on paper, it watched as other religious groups began to emerge with equal status in the new Russia.

Seeing this great new window of opportunity, responsible evangelical Christians began to establish contacts and explore ways of helping Russian Christians. Others, unencumbered by scruples and accountability, saw the situation as an opportunity for profit. Using the established needs as leverage, and with the unwitting assistance of hurting people grasping at straws, they solicited help from abroad that never reached those who needed it.

Russian Baptists saw the changes in their country as a glorious new day. Established in 1867, they predated the Bolshevik Revolution by half a century and thus were permitted to continue their existence under Communism. Persecution and restrictions had, however, taken their toll. Men in many of the Russian Baptist churches had been taken away, never to return. Many others who refused to renounce their faith were often denied basic necessities, higher education, and advancement in their work. Intimidation and poverty were constant companions of those who remained faithful in the churches.

Now, after 70 years of repression and persecution, these faithful believers enjoyed their newfound freedom to witness. Russian Baptists baptized 30,000 people in 1991—1 new Christian believer for every 10 members. Long crippled by a severe lack of resources, they now could hope for help from outside as they tried to overcome years of deprivation.

Sensitive to the needs and opportunities emerging from these extraordinary events, Southern Baptists moved quickly to establish a viable missionary presence in Russia. After serving for 34 years in career missions work in South America, George and Veda Rae Lozuk agreed to begin this new work. George had learned some of the difficult Russian language from his father, a Belarussian immigrant. With 2 years remaining before their retirement, the Lozuks moved to the largest country in the world to start this enormous new missions enterprise. By the time of their retirement in June 1993, six other couples had joined them in their work there.

Capable and committed, these missions pioneers needed orientation and training for their new place of service and time to learn the language. A small team with a huge responsibility, they also needed reinforcements who could move quickly into the areas of opportunity, establish mission points, and strengthen weak congregations. They needed people who could buy them some time as they adjusted and conserve for them precious opportunities that might otherwise be lost.

The best option was a state Baptist convention willing and able to accept what was perhaps the greatest partnership missions challenge ever. Russia was virtually uncharted in terms of missions work. The only missionaries who would be in place would be almost as new to the country as the partnership volunteers would be. For the most part, these missionaries would be unable to work directly with the volunteers.

Kentucky Baptists' successful partnership reputation with Kenya and Brazil impressed Bill Peacock, the Foreign Mission Board's representative for Russia. And he knew Bill Marshall as a capable leader with a heart for missions. Seeing the potential for a "marriage made in heaven," he offered Kentucky Baptists the challenge of a partnership in Russia.

Surely this relationship originated in the mind of God. As the window of opportunity opened in Russia and the

Foreign Mission Board moved to seize it, Kentucky Baptists rose to meet this challenge.

Though our partnership with Espirito Santo did not end until 1993, we began exploratory visits to Russia in 1992. Our two successful partnerships established this new way of doing missions as a major emphasis for the Kentucky Baptist Convention. We knew we would need a bold, new challenge if we were to continue to grow in this direction. The timing in Russia was just right.

The Lozuks and Mel and Nancy Skinner, the only missionaries in Russia at the time, coordinated our exploratory visits. Other Kentucky Baptist Convention workers making the initial trip with Bill Marshall were Benton Williams, missions and evangelism division director; and Calvin Wilkins, coordinator for the Brazil partnership.

This delegation met with Vasily Logvinyenko, president of the Russian Baptist Union; Pyotr Konovalchik, pastor of Ozerkiy Baptist Church in St. Petersburg, who would succeed Logvinyenko as president; and other Russian Baptist leaders. At first, the Russians were suspicious. The new climate of openness led to an invasion of religious movements from the West, many with ulterior motives that had hurt the Russian believers and their cause. As Konovalchik explained, "We have to digest all this. We have to decide who to hear, what to do. You can imagine we have indigestion."

Both parties needed more information and further negotiations, prompting another trip by Kentucky leaders in early 1993. The Russian leaders soon realized that these Baptists from America were not selfish opportunists. They were sincere Christians who wanted nothing more than to help Russian believers lead their country to Christ. By this time, the Russian Baptists were ready to move ahead with a partnership.

But would Kentucky Baptists as a whole accept and embrace this challenge? Going into this country that had for so long been an enemy would not be easy for some. Russian Baptists desperately needed church buildings, and these would be expensive projects. Could we afford to provide not only those resources but also the significant expense of travel to Russia? After much prayer, and strongly sensing God's leadership, Kentucky Baptist leaders were ready to take a giant step of faith.

On May 3, 1993, Bill Marshall offered an emotional and compelling challenge to the members of the Executive Board of the Kentucky Baptist Convention. He asked them to undertake "what could be the most far-reaching missions opportunity that any state convention has ever had." Summing up the feelings of those who had made the two initial trips to Russia, he said, "We left believing that the Lord had put together our hands and hearts with those of the Russian Baptist Union leadership. We left with the realization that such a partnership would require the very best of Kentucky Baptist commitment. The needs are staggering, the opportunity for us unlike anything I will ever experience again in my lifetime."

All 101 board members responded to this appeal with a commitment that could only come from a strong, clear sense of God's direction. They gave the proposal a unanimous vote of approval. Kentucky Baptists were going to Russia!

The bus had seen better days. The diesel engine idled noisily as we left the plane and crossed the stretch of tarmac under the guards' watchful eyes. Filling the bus to standing-room capacity, two guards boarding last, we moved toward the airport terminal.

More guards met us at the terminal entrance, directing us down a wide, dark stairway to a row of passport control booths. Guards again watched as we waited in line, motioning the hesitant ones forward and keeping the eager ones behind the lines marked on the floor.

Such alien surroundings could easily intimidate anyone. The airport terminal's masonry walls were designed more for function than for aesthetics. The ceiling was covered with sections of large, copper-looking tubing that reminded me of artillery shell casings. They drank the dim light, leaving the whole area poorly lit. Passengers tracked in snow, leaving wet spots all over the floor. Maintenance did not appear to be a high priority.

An acrid smoke permeated the air, issuing from oversized cigarettes many of the arriving passengers and guards smoked. Few people talked; none of them spoke English. In my previous overseas travels I had always been able to speak at least some of the native language. Here, I suddenly realized, I was in a place where I might well be unable to communicate with anyone around me. But then, that was the reason I had come.

Our 5-year partnership would begin in January 1994. The months following the convention's approval brought intense preparation and planning. Everyone was eager to begin the work as soon as possible, with two preliminary projects scheduled for late 1993. As plans took shape, a significant problem surfaced. Interpreters qualified to work with the soon-to-arrive volunteers were scarce.

Hostile relations between the United States and Russia during the cold war had prompted Communist Russia to discourage English as a second language. Most Russians who had studied English had had very little opportunity to use it in conversation. Of those who could speak English, only a very few were Baptist, and almost none had any experience as interpreters.

Missionary Norman Lytle had a solution. He and his wife, Martha, had transferred from Israel to the newly opened work in Russia in October 1992. Norman, slated to succeed George Lozuk as coordinator for the FMB's work there when the Lozuks retired the next year, proposed a school for interpreters. He envisioned Kentucky Baptist teachers training English-speaking Russian Baptists to work with future Kentucky volunteers. That's where I came in.

Enthusiasm and excitement were contagious in the meeting at which Bill Marshall challenged Kentucky Baptists to enter the partnership with Russian Baptists. I saw this as a once-in-a-lifetime opportunity, a true Macedonian call, and I knew at that moment that I would somehow become involved.

Russian Baptists envisioned starting 1,000 new churches, which would need new pastors to serve and nurture them. Of the targeted project needs, teaching new pastors seemed to match my abilities best. With 25 years' experience as a pastor, and with much of my seminary training focused on teaching, I believed God could use me in this new work.

I had discovered an affinity for languages as a high school student and pursued this in college by majoring in German. In seminary graduate studies I learned Hebrew and Greek. With that background, and having traveled in Europe and the Middle East, I felt I could communicate across cultural lines with Russia's soon-to-be pastors.

As I shared my sense of calling to this work with Calvin Wilkins, partnership coordinator, we discussed the opportunities and how I might fit into them with my gifts and abilities "down the road." I thought I would have 1 year, maybe 2, to prepare, study, and save some money for the expensive trip. God knew that these things would take time. It appeared I would soon be leaving the church I had been serving, and that transition would also delay my availability.

Or so I thought. As Calvin processed Norman Lytle's proposal for training interpreters, he remembered his conversation with me. Much sooner than I expected, in November 1993, Calvin called to ask me to go to Russia, and not for the job I had expected.

"How do you train interpreters?" I asked him.

"We don't know. We've never done it before," he replied.

"But I don't know any Russian!"

"No one else who is available does either."

"When will the project be?" I asked, hoping at least for some time to prepare.

"January of next year," he said. "Some of the people we want to train are students who will be out of school then."

Two months away! "But I'm leaving my church. I've already resigned. I can't ask them to help, and I can't afford the trip right now."

Even as I raised these objections, I began to feel that this might be God's doing. I had anticipated a job that I could do without having to depend on God so much. Maybe God wanted me to do something I absolutely couldn't do without His help.

"Yes," I said. "I'll do it. If God will provide the way, I'll do it."

"This is a critical need," Calvin continued. "We need for these interpreters to be trained soon so they can be available for the other projects we have planned for the spring. Pray about it, and I will too. We'll see what the Lord can work out."

I hung up the phone, surprised at what I had agreed to, wondering where God would take all of this. I shared this with my wife, Robbie, and a few close friends at church and asked them to pray with me about it. I felt a growing sense of God's leading in this direction, but I knew it would take a miracle.

Before a week passed, the miracle came. Virginia Downing, one of my church's strongest mission supporters, had seemed a natural to join me in prayer about this need. But I had underestimated her—and God. Virginia, never one to waste words, was short and sweet with her message when she called: "Preacher, you know that missions trip to Russia you told me about? You go on and make your plans for it. I've been on the phone with some folks and the money is all there." Speechless for a moment, I managed to thank her. I didn't know it then, but I would learn to expect many more miracles as the partnership progressed.

Three other Kentucky Baptists agreed to help train the interpreters. Peggy Kemp of Cadiz and Jane Dyer of Trenton went to St. Petersburg. Alan Chamness, a minister of music from Henderson, joined me for the school in Moscow. As I waited in line for my turn at the passport control booth, Alan's face was the only one I recognized, and his was the only voice I understood.

The guard motioned me forward. I walked to the booth, where a very serious-looking official in a military uniform said, "Passport!" in heavily accented English. As I waited, he punched at what I assumed was a computer hidden behind the shelf of his booth. He looked carefully at my face, comparing it to my passport and visa pictures. He checked the angled mirror behind me to make sure I wasn't hiding anything out of his view. Apparently satisfied, he returned my passport and visa and waved me through.

In spite of his excess baggage, Alan also made it through. In addition to his two carry-on bags he had brought along two inexpensive guitars as gifts, persuading other passengers to claim them in order to avoid exceeding the two-bag limit. After claiming our bags at the luggage carousel and loading them onto a cart, we moved to the next "green line" for customs inspection. The official carefully examined our declaration forms and counted our bags. He scribbled in the blank spaces of the forms and motioned us through. So far, no one had smiled or offered any kind of greeting. Was this the way Russians welcomed Americans?

Getting outside the customs area, where we expected someone to meet us, was another daunting experience. We waded through a sea of people, all crowding forward to meet arriving passengers, some holding signs with names on them. None bore our names. We finally got to a somewhat open area and looked around again, hoping to find someone to meet us. We had no idea whom it would be or how we would recognize them.

We waited anxiously, but no one came. Alan and I took turns waiting with the luggage while the other walked around to look for our mysterious host. I walked back through the crowd, thinking we had missed the sign bearing our names. Finally, as Alan took another turn around the area, a tall young man cautiously approached me, looking intently at the load of luggage on the cart beside me. He was holding a yellow legal pad, and as he came nearer, I saw my name on it, written in large letters. Deliverance! We had made contact with someone in this vast unknown land who knew who we were.

His name was Konstantin Stailets, Kostya for short, and he was Norman Lytle's assistant. We had been told we would stay in a hotel in Moscow, but Kostya informed us that "there has been a change." We soon learned that such changes were a way of life in Russia. Instead of a hotel, we would stay in the guest rooms at the Russian Baptist Union's newly completed building, home to the Baptist seminary. Our interpreters classes would meet there, and the interpreters attending the classes would stay there as well. The location was convenient for everyone.

The drive from the airport took most of an hour. In spite of the jet lag, the sight of Moscow at night awed me. The Moscow River, the Kremlin, Red Square—it all somehow seemed unreal. Yet I was actually here, on a Christian mission in this atheistic country. Silently I prayed that God would keep me focused and help me to be faithful to His purpose amid all that could distract me.

Because of our late arrival, Norman had instructed Kostya to take us to eat before we went to our quarters. We drove through the heart of Moscow; then Kostya pulled the car into a parking place. We walked around a corner only to be greeted by the familiar golden arches of a

McDonald's restaurant, one of three in Moscow at that time. Except for the menu written in Russian, everything looked the same as back home. And the food tasted just the same. So much for our first Russian meal!

By the time we finally arrived at the Russian Baptist Union, it was too late to really see what it looked like. Kostya escorted us to the third floor and helped us get our luggage upstairs. Halfway down the hall, a door opened into a kind of foyer that served three separate sleeping rooms and a common two-room bath. Unlocking one of the sleeping rooms, he motioned us inside, where we saw two narrow beds, a combination writing-dining table, and a wardrobe. It looked adequate for either of us. When Alan asked which of the other rooms was ours, a puzzled look came over Kostya's face. Holding up two fingers, he looked at the beds. "Two people, two beds. It is logical," he said. And that was that. This would be home for the next two incredible weeks.

2

WELCOME TO RUSSIA!

It didn't smell like breakfast. I couldn't determine what it was, but it certainly didn't smell like bacon and eggs, or anything else to which I was accustomed for my morning meal. *Flexibility.* That was the word in orientation. I was eager to see what smelled so different.

I was hungry enough to try anything. An early riser anyway, I had been awake since 3:00 A.M., thanks to the effect of the 8-hour time difference. The narrow bed and rough sheets had been comfortable enough, but I had fought the pillow for more sleep until the rooster crowed—in the heart of Moscow!—around 5:00 A.M.

Alan still snored in the next bed. Throughout the night, I had heard someone entering and leaving one of the other nearby rooms. This seemed a good time to bathe, dress, and get out of the way of those who could sleep. Not knowing if our neighbor was male or female, I put on some clothes, gathered my supplies, and headed for the common bathroom. Russians typically have two-room bathrooms, with one room for the toilet and the other for the lavatory and shower or tub. This arrangement has definite advantages, especially when, as is usually the case, several people share the facilities.

After finally figuring out that the little knob on the top of the toilet tank had to be pulled up to flush, I headed for the other room. As I began to brush my teeth, I remembered that I wasn't supposed to drink the water. I made a mental note to rinse my toothbrush later, after I had boiled some water. I was ready for a shave, but I noticed the lavatory had no stopper. As luck would have it, the top for my travel-sized shaving lather fit almost perfectly.

My next challenge was the shower: a square, porcelain fixture only six inches high, with no enclosure or curtain. The handheld showerhead was attached to a hose, but there seemed to be no way to keep from splattering the floor. A thin, wooden lattice device, something I was obviously intended to stand on, lay against the wall. But should I place it inside the shower, or outside? In, I decided, although after trying it I changed my mind. By keeping the water flow very low I managed not to get the floor too wet, which was a good thing, considering the only towel I had been given was a 1-by-2-foot rectangle. And as I later learned, I was expected to use this one towel for the entire two weeks! Russia was going to be interesting, I thought. Little did I know!

With an hour before breakfast time, I decided to look around the place I would eat, sleep, and work for the next two weeks. The building looked much older than I knew it actually was. Completed just three months before my arrival, the Russian Baptist Union headquarters was reportedly the first building constructed by Baptists in Moscow in over 100 years.

Including basement and attic, the building had six floors. The walls were thick masonry, brick on the exterior and plastered concrete on interior walls and ceilings. Pipes jutted from the walls at odd places to supply the plumbing fixtures and heating radiators. Electrical wiring was embedded in the plaster without conduit. The floors, an ill-fitting herringbone pattern, were hardwood except for the bathrooms, which had large, ornate ceramic tiles with coarse joints. The building's furnishings were institutional in quality and style. I wondered why a new building would look like this. I would later learn that this was the norm for much of Russia, for reasons that would define many other facets of the country's culture.

His name was Andrei, and he appeared to be very shy. I introduced myself when we met in the hallway. He spoke passable English in a soft, baritone voice. He looked to be in his mid-30s, of average height, with thinning red hair and a wispy beard surrounding his pleasant but stoic face. He was one of our students in the interpreters school. He and some of the others had arrived the night before, even though the school would not begin until the next day.

As we talked, another Russian appeared. His name was Alexander. About Andrei's age, he was shorter and wore thick glasses. He spoke English well, and was more assertive than Andrei. Alan joined us, and the two Russians escorted us to our first real Russian meal in the dining room of the Russian Baptist Union.

Two *babushkas*—the word means "grandmother" but is typically used for any older women—stood behind a small serving table, ladling hot cereal into bowls for people as they came in. I didn't recognize the cereal, but it smelled good.

As we seated ourselves at one of the tables, I noticed that all of the tables held serving plates of bread and cheese. We helped ourselves to utensils from another table, and Alexander brought a kettle from the same table and served us hot tea. Our table also held a plate of butter and a dish of coarse sugar, but neither had a serving utensil. Realizing that the etiquette might be different, I waited for the Russians to lead the way. I soon discovered that one's own utensils, even those already used for eating, were used for common dishes.

The breads, some dark and some white, were coarse and tasty. The cereal, millet with milk and sugar, was also quite tasty and with the bread and cheese made a satisfying meal. Then I noticed that others went back for plates of different food. Andrei and Alexander led the way as we removed our cereal bowls and again got in line, this time for a boiled wiener served with fried potatoes and onions and slices of tomatoes and cucumbers.

Typical Russian cuisine, I discovered, is usually simple food served in abundance. Choice is limited and often dictated by what is available in the markets. Russians plan their menus after they shop. But the food is usually good and always served with gracious hospitality. Though many of the dishes are unfamiliar to Americans, they are quite delicious.

During the next two weeks, and over the course of 5 years and seven trips to Russia, I would spend a total of four months in this country, and I would come to love it very deeply. The experience would change my life profoundly. I would work with well over 1,000 volunteers to Russia, sharing their experiences through conversations and written evaluations they would submit following their projects. I would learn much about the country and its people, and everything I learned only made me realize how much more there was to know.

In no way do I consider myself an expert on Russia. The observations I share through these pages are perceptions that are my realities. Some of my observations come from studies prompted by the desire to know this land and these people better in order to minister to them more effectively, and to help volunteers do that as well. Other observations come from the very best sources—the Russian people themselves. Russians appear to be reserved at first meeting; but when they learn to trust you, which they do quickly, they are very generous with their friendship.

Of all the friends Russia gave me, the best are those students who worked so diligently through four interpreters schools, the first which Alan and I taught, and three later ones I taught with my wife, Robbie. Models of dedication and commitment, these students never tired of their studies in English and their interpretation drills, eagerly absorbing everything we could think to teach them.

Training these students proved to be one of the wisest decisions we made during this partnership. They quickly learned skills that would enhance the work of every project we undertook. But more than that, they were my teachers. Through their eyes and their generous sharing of experiences, I came to know Russia far better than I could have learned from all the books.

Knowing that Russia is the world's largest country makes it no easier to comprehend its enormous size. A traveler flying from the eastern coast of the United States to Moscow, in the far western part of Russia, crosses 8 time zones. That same traveler, flying across Russia from Moscow to the country's easternmost tip near Alaska, crosses 11 time zones. Russia's land area is almost twice that of the United States. Its very size creates a host of problems: transportation, communication, and governmental efficiency, to name a few. It seems to be much too large to be just one country.

Russia's climate varies widely, from extreme cold and ice in the north to periods of extreme heat in the south. Oppressive snow in the winter melts and creates a season of mud in the spring. In their invasions of Russia, both Napoleon and Hitler were stopped in no small part by this unfriendly climate.

As diverse as Russia is in climate and topography, even more diverse is the ethnic and cultural background of its people. So broadly does this land cover its continent that it is common to speak of European Russia and Asian Russia. For many centuries in its development, large land areas and numerous people groups came under Russian rule. Instead of one vast nation, Russia is in many ways more like a cluster of different nations.

Although it is among the world's richest nations in natural resources, much of this treasure lies in Russia's sparsely populated northern areas and is difficult to develop because of the severe climate. As knowledge of and technology for mining these resources grew, a Communist government that owned everything offered no reward for such development and thus allowed Russia's economy to deteriorate with incredible wealth begging to emerge.

From Cimmerians to Huns to Slavs to Tatars to Mongols, Russia's ancient history reads like an Old Testament list of tribes Israel encountered. It is a colorful parade of European and Asian cultures. The 1300s saw the decline of the Mongols, the rise of the Russian princes, and the consolidation of much of the territories that would make Russia the vast country it became. In 1547, Ivan IV—Ivan the Terrible—took the title of czar and thus began a period of absolute power for the ruling class. For the next 300 years, the peasants were bound to the land in serfdom, and Russia followed a path divergent from the rest of Western European culture. Not until 1861 were the serfs freed.

Under the czars, Russia continued with such notable figures as Peter the Great, who brought much Western European influence into the country. He founded St. Petersburg, and in 1712, moved the capital there from Moscow. In the latter part of that century under Catherine the Great, Russia joined the ranks of major world powers. The 1800s saw Russia defeat Napoleon's army and expand Russian rule into much of Asia.

Basic to an understanding of Russia is the knowledge that most Russians, even today, have little or no concept of ownership. In American culture, we take for granted the freedom to buy and own goods almost at will. For most Americans, owning homes and businesses is, if not a present reality, at least a reasonable aspiration. This simple but profound cultural difference results in radically differing views about things like individual rights, responsibilities, and laws.

Traffic laws, for example, are a matter of disdain for many Russians. Robbie and I experienced this reality on our first visit to the 900-year-old city of Ryazan. Viktor and Violette had invited us to spend Saturday night with them, their daughter, and Violette's mother in their apartment. Gracious hosts, they prepared a sumptuous meal following our 11:00 P.M. arrival by train. On Sunday morning we were going to the Baptist church in Ryazan, where I would preach in the worship service.

Although he was not a member of the church, Viktor wanted to drive us there for the service. After going to get his car from its protective garage some distance away, he pulled up to the front of the apartment to pick us up. Robbie got into the backseat with Violette and her mother, and I took the front passenger seat. Russian law requires the use of seat belts, and I began to fasten mine. "Nyet!" Viktor spoke no English and motioned for me simply to drape the belt across my lap so that it would appear to be fastened.

I smiled and fastened it anyway, and we started on our journey to the church. Soon we turned onto a wide, straight, four-lane boulevard, and Viktor increased his speed—too much, as Russian men like to do. I saw the police car parked beside the road, but it was too late. The policeman pointed his black-and-white baton toward us and motioned us over. Muttering something in Russian, Viktor reached into his glove compartment and retrieved his documents and wallet. There would be no mercy. He would pay the fine on the spot—in cash.

In a few minutes he returned to the car, keenly aware of the presence of his wife, his mother-in-law, and his two American guests, and we drove off again. Robbie, with more than her usual naivete, asked, "What's the matter? Did we do something wrong?"

In broken English, Violette exclaimed, "He go quickly! Alla time I tell him not go quickly, and he no listen!" Somehow I'm sure that, even without knowing English, Viktor understood her.

Viktor's disdain for the seat belt and speed laws is typical of the culture of reasonable disobedience Russians learned to display under the myriad laws Communism brought. Russian law requires citizens to carry passports even in their own country. They must frequently show them for identification. Once while conducting an interpreters school in St. Petersburg, Robbie and I went to afternoon tea with Valeriy, one of the students. He and his cousin, Svetlana, also a student, lived on the island of Kronshtadt, which lies in the Gulf of Finland, in the middle of a long causeway linking it to the mainland on both sides.

After class, Valeriy and Svetlana picked us up in his car, and we started toward Kronshtadt. As we headed out across the causeway, I asked about the unusual location of the town. They explained that it was a naval fortress where Russian ships were berthed, and that the causeway was a barrier to protect the harbor from invasion. The only people living there worked at the naval installation. Then I asked a question I should have asked much earlier: "Are visitors allowed in such a sensitive military installation?"

"Visitors are only allowed with special permission, and then only if you have family there," Svetlana replied.

"Then how will we get in?" I asked.

"No problem," Valeriy responded, using this favorite expression of Russians who speak English. "We get in by showing our passports. This morning I borrowed two passports for you from friends who were not going anywhere."

I was getting very uncomfortable. I had not intended to break any laws or go anywhere I was not supposed to go.

But the causeway road had no place to turn around. I remembered that Valeriy was a ship's pilot and Svetlana was an attorney. Before long we could need the services of one or both of them.

"How will we be able to use someone else's passport?" I asked. "They will have the wrong pictures."

"No problem," Valeriy assured us again. "They do not look at the picture, only the address in the back." He handed us the passports, opened to the back cover where an address was handwritten in each one.

At that moment we approached a guardhouse with its crossing gate lowered. I could envision Robbie and me trying to explain this situation to Russian military authorities, and it was not a pleasant thought. "You only must hold the picture up to the car window," Valeriy said. "Do not smile and do not speak."

We did as he told us. The guards glanced our direction from some ten feet away and waved us through. I breathed a deep sigh of relief as we handed the borrowed passports back to Valeriy.

"Keep them," he said. "You will need them when we return to St. Petersburg."

We would see such attitudes many times over the years of our partnership, even among some of the Christians. It is accepted practice in their culture, and not a moral issue. Riding the bus for a short distance without paying the fare seemed to them a reasonable risk, like jaywalking in America. Several times I accepted their offer to take my money and buy my train tickets and admission tickets before I realized they were getting me the Russian price. Because they considered the higher price for me unfair, they had no qualms about circumventing the rule. Like Kentucky Baptists, Russian Christians have developed cultural habits and practices that may appear to others to compromise their faith.

Christianity entered the pages of Russian history shortly before A.D. 1000, when Grand Prince Vladimir I became a Christian. He made Christianity the state religion, and most of what was then Russia followed his lead. The Russian Orthodox Church came to dominate the religious scene and did much to shape the developing Russian culture. It has changed little over the centuries, but since the fall of Communism it has been trying to reassert its state church status. Without a Reformation similar to those that gave rise to Protestantism in other countries, religions other than Russian Orthodoxy have had to swim against the tide to gain a foothold in Russia. Baptists have been more successful than most. Chapter 3 explores some of their history and development.

Czars led Russia into the twentieth century, but their rule did not last long after that. For over 300 years, the lavish excesses of this ruling class had come at the expense of the peasants. Reforms in recent times had not gone far enough to alleviate their poverty, leaving the situation ripe for revolution, even a bad one. In 1914, embroiled in World War I, Russia found herself unable to meet the needs of her troops in battle and her people at home. Severe shortages of basic goods heightened the people's dissatisfaction with the czar.

In 1917, Vladimir Ilyich Lenin led the Bolshevik Revolution, ending the era of the czars and ushering in the age of Communism. His rule, and that of others like Joseph Stalin who followed him, proved to be even more disastrous for the people who had sought relief in his ideology. Though Lenin died after a brief 7 years in power, the radical changes he and his successors brought about defined

Russian history until the fall of Communism and the end of the Soviet Union in 1991.

The icy wind whipped the light snow in swirls around the onion spires of the Cathedral of St. Basil, sending waves of white dancing across the cobblestoned expanse of Red Square. A slippery crust made for hazardous walking, and the large, open area separating the Kremlin Wall and GUM, the 100-year-old shopping mall, was all but deserted. Guards stood at attention outside the doorway to the massive marble facade of Lenin's Tomb, built in the shadow of the Kremlin Wall. It was January 1994, and Lenin was suddenly out of official favor. Whether from the blustery cold or the change in political climate, there was no line of people waiting to enter this historic edifice, although an occasional brave soul going in indicated that it was open.

"Let's see if we can go in," I said to Misha, my student interpreter and guide from the city of Kimri, 100 miles north of Moscow. We made our way across to the tomb and I gestured toward the door with a questioning expression. A guard nodded, so we walked inside. The black marble walls soaked up most of the light, making it difficult to see. Another guard instructed me to remove my hat and motioned us down a wide stairway and into the tomb area, completely underground.

At the foot of the stairs we turned right, toward an area that seemed to have a bit more light. Then I saw the light's source, the only light inside the building. It came from directly over the body of Vladimir Ilyich Lenin, enclosed in a glass coffin. He had died 70 years ago that month, but the body was as well preserved as if he had died the day before. We made our way slowly around a low wall that kept visitors at a respectful distance but allowed viewing from three sides. However much this man may have believed his plans would lead Russia to its days of glory, his disastrous legacy, under which Russia now struggled, had proved beyond all doubt the folly of planning without God.

We took a different stairway back up and out a side exit into the bitter January cold. Somehow, it didn't seem as cold as the place we had just been.

"Well, what was your impression?" I asked. Misha was 25, the son of the pastor of the Baptist church in Kimri, and himself a Christian believer since the age of 18. He had grown up under Communism, learning the atheistic doctrine in school. He had also suffered through the economic failure of Communism and experienced additional hardships imposed upon Christians by Russia's Marxist dictators. Misha had never before been inside Lenin's Tomb. I wondered how the experience had affected him.

"It was nothing," he said quietly with a shrug of his shoulders.

Four months later Robbie and I were again in Moscow. It was a beautiful spring day. As we walked inside the Kremlin with a group of student interpreters in a square bursting with new flowers, a huge granite statue of a seated Lenin looked benignly toward the Kremlin palace. Denis, a young kindergarten teacher from Smolensk, looked intently at the statue. He seemed to be in deep thought as I walked over to join him. In a voice heavy with exasperation he said, "That man! When I was a boy he was like a god. Now he is . . . nothing!"

Nothing, indeed. But the economic chaos that accompanied Lenin's disastrous social experiment still threatens to suck Russia down in a whirlpool of ideologies and pressures competing for her soul. After a turbulent decade of *perestroika* (restructuring) and *glasnost* (openness), Russia shows little indication of finding her way in the twenty-first century. The beginning of a free-market economy triggered runaway inflation that left money worthless. Privatization of businesses and the opportunity to buy state-owned residences have fallen prey to organized crime and widespread corruption, the sorry offspring of failed Communism and a dispossessed KGB (state secret police).

The Metro, Moscow's efficient subway system, works well by necessity. Some estimates claim that as many as 12,000,000 riders use it daily, making it essential to Muscovites and those in other places who depend on what happens in Moscow. The railway system, which accounts for most Russian travel, also works well. Too much else, however, does not work. Many who learned under Communism that there was no connection between how well you work and how much you earn have not learned that a free-market economy cannot allow that philosophy.

Good roads are important in any country, but especially so in a country as big as Russia. Outside the Moscow area, the country's roads are usually in poor condition. As another Misha drove us from a school in St. Petersburg to our apartment, he grew weary of trying to dodge huge potholes. "In Russia," he said, "we don't have roads; we have directions!" Placing that observation alongside a highway sign I saw presents a daunting picture of auto travel in Russia. The sign read, Ryazan 78. Chelyabinsk 1818.

The distances are in kilometers, and the latter equals approximately 1,130 miles!

The government, by far Russia's largest employer, is broke. People are often not paid for months at a time, but they are afraid to give up their jobs because millions of unemployed people are waiting for them. It is not uncommon to hear Russians express at least a tentative desire to return to Communism. Things were bad, they reason, but at least under Communism everyone had a job, something so important for one's identity in Russia; and everyone had an income, meager though it might be.

This was the country, the climate, the culture, the condition into which Kentucky Baptists plunged, sure of God's call to help bring the good news of Jesus Christ to a people who needed it as much as ever any people did. It was an impossible task that would draw out of us more than we had to give, and teach us a new level of dependence upon God.

As we joined hands with Baptists in Russia, we would also learn firsthand how God had sustained His people in times and circumstances more difficult than most of us would ever know.

Interpreters school, January 1994: *Foreground,* author; *left to right,* Ghennady Razumov, David Gabrielian, Misha Petrov, Andrei Nikolayev.

Interpreters school, March 1995: Andrei Nikolayev interprets for Ken Murphy.

3

THE MOST PERNICIOUS SECT

At the heart of Kentucky Baptists' work in Russia were project coordinators Larry and Joy Lindsey, Lee and Sarah Bivins, and Bob and Nancy Walden. The Lindseys arrived in Moscow in February 1994 after leaving Plum Creek Baptist Church near Taylorsville. The Bivinses, retired career missionaries from Mt. Vernon, moved to St. Petersburg the next month to coordinate the work there. The following year the Waldens, retired from business in Louisville, joined the Lindseys in Moscow.

Each went to Russia expecting culture shock, expecting to work under difficult circumstances with people who often would be unresponsive and even hostile. While they knew a core of Russian Baptist believers existed, they did not anticipate the incredible depth of faith and level of commitment these fellow believers had.

Shortly after arriving in Moscow, Joy Lindsey went to tea with Russian Baptists involved in women's work and International Mission Board (IMB; formerly Foreign Mission Board) missionaries. There she heard a moving testimony from Tamara, one of the women's work leaders from

Moscow. Tamara told the group about another group of women who faithfully attend every service at Central Baptist Church in Moscow, four or five services each week. Relying on public transportation to reach the church, some of them travel more than 2 hours to get there. Before each service, these women gather to pray for God's blessing and movement in that service. For more than 10 years these women had prayed daily for God to send help and spiritual revival to Russia.

It had not been easy for them. They were all older women. Many were widows whose husbands, refusing to deny their Christian faith, had been forcefully taken from their homes and either executed or exiled to Siberian labor camps, where they later died. And because they were also Christians, these widows were often denied their customary benefits and pensions. Yet they had remained strong in their faith, praying that one day Russians would be free to attend church openly and practice their religion unhindered by atheistic restrictions.

God had answered their prayers. Before Kentucky Baptists even considered plans for a partnership with Baptists in Russia, they had prayed for help. And now their prayers were being answered. The long-term ministry of IMB missionaries and the more immediate ministry of Kentucky Baptist volunteers had converged in Russia for God's use, again demonstrating God's faithfulness to His people.

The path Russian Baptists traveled during the 70 years of Communist rule had been difficult. Most of us could not comprehend the persecution and hardship these dedicated believers had suffered.

Baptists in Russia date their beginning to August 20, 1867, when Nikita Voronin was baptized under cover of darkness. Their numbers grew rapidly, gaining momentum with the Bolshevik Revolution in 1917, as Lenin decreed a separation of church and state. That very growth became a threat to the success of this atheistic movement, however, and in the 1930s Stalin's bloody purges decimated their ranks. This murderous persecution abated later, but it took other forms during the remainder of the Communist era.

Valter Mitskevich, now retired after a distinguished career in Russian Baptist life, served as a minister in Central Baptist Church in Moscow and as superintendent of Baptist work in the Tver region. Highly respected as a scholar and Baptist statesman, he studied at Spurgeon's College in London for 2 years and is fluent in English. On a long trip to Seltzo, south of Moscow, he told me some of his story.

Born in 1931 in Gorky (now Nizhni Novgorod), Valter felt the pain of Stalin's purges early. In 1934, his father was arrested for the "crime" of being a minister. He was sent first to Kazakhstan to work in a coal mine, and later to a concentration camp in Siberia. His family barely survived, but Valter's father maintained his strong commitment to God. He lived until he was 83, preaching his last sermon just a week before his death. Valter vividly remembers the hunger of his early years, even today sometimes waking to hear his childhood voice crying, "I am hungry. Give me bread."

After high school, Valter pursued a career in medicine and was admitted to dental school. In order to succeed in his career, he was pressured into joining the Komsomol—the Communist youth organization. While working in St. Petersburg he met a group of young Christians and was "converted altogether" at age 24. He returned to Moscow, compelled to confess his faith to his Komsomol superiors, who immediately revoked his diploma and thus ended his medical career. Painful as that was, Valter considers it God's way of directing him into his ministry vocation.

Christian believers were routinely denied basic rights and privileges when Communist authorities learned of their faith. And their own religious convictions denied them other benefits. Living *na levo* (to the left) became accepted practice in Russian society, as people depended on the black market and bribery to get many of the things they needed. Because their beliefs refused to let them cheat, Russian Christians were often unable to obtain things like building materials and furnishings that were regularly in short supply. In spite of the consequences, these faithful believers maintained their witness. They sometimes suffered serious deprivation, even martyrdom. Even in those terrible times, vindication occasionally came to those who stood fast in their faith.

Alexei Markhin is a pastor in beautiful Nizhni Novgorod, Russia's third largest city, situated on the Volga River. After morning and noontime worship services at two different churches one Sunday, I spent an enjoyable afternoon with Pastor Markhin; his wife, Maria; their children; and their grandchildren. Both in their mid-60s, the senior Markhins had lived through the dreadful Communist years. I listened intently as they recalled their lives during those days.

Schoolchildren who were Christian believers were publicly ridiculed, and teachers challenged their faith in the classroom. Once when a teacher insisted that atheistic evolution was the only explanation for the origin of humans, a student maintained his belief in creation. The teacher said, "Then you are the son of Adam? You will be called Adamovich!"

The student replied, "Then you are descended from a monkey? You should be called Obezyanovich (son of a monkey)." The other students laughed and pounced on the name with such delight that eventually the teacher was forced to leave the school because of their mockery.

After finishing high school, Maria Markhin went to the university to prepare for a career as a teacher. One year short of receiving her degree, the Communist authorities learned she was a Christian believer. "We cannot trust you with our children," they said. "You must pass an examination in atheism. You must choose between your God and your university degree."

Refusing to renounce her faith, Maria was not allowed to continue her university studies. Even after all the intervening years since that day, tears from that painful memory came to Maria's eyes as she recalled that experience. She reflected a moment; then her eyes brightened. "That was during the time of Khrushchev. He said, 'Soon there will be no more Christians.' Now Khrushchev is gone, and we are still here!"

Indeed! On another day I strolled through the restricted area between Lenin's Tomb and the Kremlin Wall, viewing the graves and monuments of so many prominent figures from the Communist years. Plaques affixed to the Kremlin Wall memorialize some. Sculpted busts and huge gravestones mark the time in Soviet history of others. But Nikita Khrushchev, who had fallen into disfavor in later years, had been purged from Soviet history, his remains taken away from their prestigious resting place. Curious to know what the official comment would be, I asked a guard where Khrushchev was buried.

"Khrushchev nyet," he replied, looking away.

Kentucky Baptists arrived in Russia at the dawn of a new day. Leonid Kotelnikov served as administrative assistant for the Kentucky Baptist partnership office in Moscow. Active with his wife and sons at Moscow's Central Baptist Church, he could easily recall a time when his family would not have been able to attend church together. As a small boy, he had been denied entrance to this same church, forced by Communist KGB agents to stay outside with other children while his mother went in to worship.

Shortly after the Lytles arrived in Moscow, they attended worship at Leonid's church. Martha recalled that, following singing by the children's choir, a Russian woman stood and prayed aloud. With tears rolling down her face, she thanked God for granting them this new freedom they now enjoyed and for the blessing of being able to hear young people singing God's praises in His church.

Perhaps the greatest irony of the history of Russian Baptists is the face of their persecutor today. Almost from their beginning in this country, these Christians have lived with open hostility and misrepresentation by the Russian Orthodox Church. Those who should have most welcomed their fervent evangelism and generous humanitarianism instead have consistently tried to undermine their effectiveness and eliminate their influence. They view Baptists and other evangelicals as sects, dissenters from the official church.

Russian Orthodoxy, the country's largest denomination, has had its share of persecution as well. Begun as a state religion, it has maintained this status throughout much of its history. Compromise became a byword over the centuries as it accommodated pagan custom and political dictum in order to keep its privileged place. But as Peter the Great and his successors brought Western influence into Russia, the authority of the conservative Orthodox Church was sharply curtailed.

With the decline of the czars, the church's star began to rise once more. But in 1917, the Bolshevik Revolution again reversed its fortunes. On the one hand, it exposed the spiritual bankruptcy of this religion of convenience. As Lenin's Communists came to power, Holy Russia, as the Russian Orthodox Church called her, suddenly became an officially atheistic nation. On the other hand, the fate of what had been the most powerful religious body in Russia now matched that of Baptists and other minority religious groups.

The once privileged Russian Orthodoxy clergy and parishioners were persecuted along with those of other faiths. Of the 50,000 priests and 163 bishops before the revolution, just over 100 priests and 7 bishops remained as World War II began. The Stalin years were the worst. In the 1930s, in Moscow alone, all but 100 of 600 Russian Orthodox churches were closed. Many were destroyed, including the most famous one in all of Orthodoxy.

In 1813, to commemorate Russia's victory over Napoleon the previous year, Czar Alexander I ordered the building of a magnificent Russian Orthodox cathedral. With sacrificial gifts from peasants across the country, the Cathedral of Christ the Savior was completed in 1883. Standing on a hill on the bank of the Moscow River, this beautiful 30-story structure dominated the city's skyline, easily viewed from the Kremlin. It was the largest Orthodox church in the world, proclaiming the preeminence of Orthodox religion in Russia. In 1931, less than a half-century after its completion, Stalin ordered the cathedral dynamited and plundered the wreckage.

The same glasnost that now affords Baptists such freedom in Russia has, of course, opened the door for everyone else. The Russian Orthodox Church, already restored to much of its state church status in the later years of Communism, continues to reassert its dominance in the new Russia.

In 1995, a $500 million reconstruction project on the Cathedral of Christ the Savior was begun on the same site as the original, backed by Moscow mayor Yuri Luzhkov and Russian president Boris Yeltsin. After perhaps the fastest construction project in Russia's history, the outside was completed in time for Moscow's 850th anniversary in 1997. This Orthodox showpiece, built in the midst of Russia's severe economic crisis, and, many say, with tax revenues diverted from far more pressing human needs, stands as a testimony to the influence that Russian Orthodoxy has and intends to maintain.

As the government acknowledges this monopolistic church, so also the church tends to fall in line behind whomever rules the Kremlin. The patriarch of the Russian Orthodox Church all but endorsed Boris Yeltsin when he campaigned for reelection in 1996. Observers speculate, however, that he would have embraced whomever won in order to continue this symbiotic but unholy alliance.

For Baptists especially, this is not a good sign. A 1995 brochure published in Moscow under the imprimatur of Alexi II, Patriarch of the Russian Orthodox Church, labels Baptists as "The Most Pernicious Sect." It offers a detailed listing of points of disagreement such as infant baptism, praying for the dead, and veneration of saints, relics, and icons. With distortion and misrepresentation, it portrays Baptists as blasphemous heretics out to deceive the weak and destroy the true faith.

Baptist history does not lack for examples of what can happen if the Russian Orthodox Church has its way. Throughout Russia, Baptists tell of discrimination fostered by Russian Orthodox priests in local communities. Baptists are often denied building permits without proper reason. People are warned not to associate with Baptists or attend their services, under threat of excommunication. Orthodox priests have even told people that Baptists sacrifice children and drink blood in their services. In an even more extreme example, an interpreter from Penza told how years earlier her grandfather had been exiled for refusing to kiss the priest's ring.

These attempts at suppression took a more sinister form in 1997. President Boris Yeltsin signed into law a controversial bill long sought by the Orthodox Church and supported by hard-line nationalists. News reports quoted Patriarch Alexei II as expressing alarm at the flood of "dangerous alien religions" which posed a threat "not only for the church but also for the state." The bill established the Russian Orthodox Church as the preeminent religion in Russia and restricted the work of other religious groups.

Russian Baptists have never had it easy, and with the economic crisis and the resurgence of power by the Russian Orthodox Church, the future no doubt holds even more difficult times. Yet these Christians maintain a resiliency and determination that enable them to move ahead with remarkable optimism. More often than not, things do not work; people do not show up on time; plans must be changed; yet Russians, both Christians and non-Christians, seem able to take all this in stride with an attitude reflected in their dismissive remark, "This is Russia."

On my first visit to Russia, I planned to attend a meeting of the only Rotary Club in Moscow. Norman Lytle had accepted the invitation to go as my guest, thinking this would be a good opportunity to meet some Muscovites outside the usual church circles. He had already mastered the difficult task of driving in Moscow traffic and knew the Russian language fairly well.

From my Rotary Club in Glasgow, Kentucky, I had obtained the address and phone number of the meeting place, a restaurant in the heart of the city. Ana, Norman's Russian secretary, had called and gotten detailed directions for us. It was an evening meeting, and the short January day had long since darkened when we set out. We allowed ourselves an hour to make the trip through the snow-covered streets, find one of the rare Moscow parking spaces, and make it to the meeting on time.

Arriving in good time, we located a parking space some two blocks from where we judged the restaurant to be. It was bitter cold, and snow fell as we walked. We could not find the restaurant. Russia's city blocks are big, and some businesses are often located behind the buildings of other businesses, reached by winding alleys. We searched the nearby area, but still no restaurant. By this time, most businesses were closed; only a few shops remained open.

We began a routine that became comical after a while. We would go into a shop and Norman would ask directions, giving the name of the restaurant. The person he asked would not be sure but would send us away with tentative instructions. We would follow them to the end, only to find nothing there that looked like the restaurant. Finally, after more than an hour of searching, we located the restaurant downstairs in what looked like an office building. We had passed it several times, but there was no sign to indicate the restaurant was there.

A nicely dressed man greeted us at the door and told us the restaurant was closed. When Norman asked him about the Rotary Club meeting, he told us they no longer met there. He graciously gave us directions to their new location, a half hour away on the other side of Moscow. Since it was already well after time for the meeting to start, and knowing that we might have the same difficulty finding the new location, we decided to give up.

We were tired and hungry, and Martha was not expecting us for dinner, so we set out to find a place to eat. Norman led us to a place he had eaten before, a walk-up, sidewalk kiosk with two small, stand-up tables. With little business at this late hour, the tables were covered with four inches of snow. We ordered two fat Russian sausages with bread and a one-liter bottle of cola with two cups. We cleared some of the snow from a table and, after giving God thanks for good fellowship and what we had learned, we laughed at the whole experience, so typical it might be repeated many times on any given day. This is Russia!

Perhaps it is this inherent adversity permeating all of Russian society that creates in the people a sense of desperate need for something meaningful, something their society will never be able to provide. By contrast, Americans enjoy a sort of culturally religious society that may allow people to feel satisfied by providing just enough of what they want that they stop looking further for the rest that is the best.

Whatever the reason, the Russian Christians I came to know impressed me with a depth of faith and commitment to discipleship that challenged me to a deeper walk of faith. That influence began with the first group of student interpreters.

Rooms were scarce in the Russian Baptist Union building, and our classroom by day became the sleeping quarters for the six male students at night. Classes lasted all day, but after dinner the men would invite us to their room for tea and more study and translation practice. They never seemed to tire of what we were doing, always eager to learn more.

Alexei, a nuclear engineering student, was so taken with my Russian-English dictionary of religious terms that he spent hours each night copying words and meanings that were new to him. David, a 16-year-old high school student and Armenian refugee from Azerbaijan, spent his spare time between class sessions reading his Bible. A new believer, he gave me a picture of his baptism the summer before. Ghennady, a retired mining engineer, struggled mightily with English. Often we had to resort to the German we both knew in order to understand each other. The women also studied after hours with the help of Tatiana Soboleva, an English literature major who assisted us in all our interpreters schools.

Each day we drilled the students in new vocabulary related to the various kinds of projects we would be doing. Alan taught them songs to break the monotony. We told them about America and Kentucky. I preached and Alan taught Bible studies they took turns interpreting from English to Russian. Then we asked one of them to speak in Russian and another to interpret into English. As each day ended, Alan and I were exhausted, but they wanted to learn more, and we couldn't refuse them. With a never-ending supply of hot Russian tea to keep us awake, we seldom left their room before midnight.

Alan and I had planned to take all of the interpreters to McDonald's for dinner when we finished the school. None had ever eaten there, and we thought it would be a fitting treat as we finished the last class on Friday. On Thursday, however, they asked if we could change our plan. Instead of going to McDonald's, they wanted to do something in our classroom.

We agreed, and after dinner that Friday we went to the classroom as they had instructed us. The room held an assortment of cookies, candy, and juice, as well as the tea Russians can't seem to do without. Our first thought was that they had planned a party for us. We soon learned that it was Natasha's birthday and, according to Russian custom, she had arranged a party for everyone, buying all the food and drinks herself.

Natasha, a pharmacist from Ryazan, was celebrating her 37th birthday. Married and the mother of two daughters, one of whom has cerebral palsy, she had been a leader in the Komsomol (the Communist youth organization) during the later years of the Communist era. She had been rewarded for her faithful service with a vacation trip to

Cuba. Just two months before our interpreters school, she had become a Christian and was awaiting baptism.

Later in the evening I thanked Natasha for having the party and inviting us to come. She explained that it was something she very much wanted to do. "My birthday is not until next week," she said. "But this is my first time to celebrate it as a believer, and I wanted to celebrate it with my brothers and sisters in Christ."

They did not know whom God would send or when it would be, but a faith such as that of the Russian Baptists expects God to answer their prayers. They expected us. And Kentucky Baptists did a great work in our 5-year partnership with Russian Baptists, but none of it would have been possible without them, our wonderful brothers and sisters in Christ. They were already hard at work and waiting expectantly for God's miracle. How blessed we were to be chosen as part of the answer to their prayers.

Left to right: Ken Murphy with Joy and Larry Lindsey, partnership coordinators in Moscow.

Valter Mitskevich interpreting for Ken Murphy in Seltzo

Maria and Alexei Markhin

Rear view of Second Baptist Church, Nizhni Novgorod

4

PEOPLE TO PEOPLE

Any concerns by Kentucky Baptist leaders that volunteers might be reluctant to venture into this once-feared country were soon dispelled. Even before we had scheduled the first projects, people began inquiring about the possibilities, sensing the same calling to go to Russia our leaders had felt. Their response was overwhelming. Believing that this might be a small window of opportunity God had given us, Kentucky Baptists eagerly began to fill the requests for project volunteers.

Partnership director Benton Williams brought 12 years of career mission service in Thailand to his work with Kentucky Baptists. He led in crafting a bold vision for this partnership. In the summer of 1993, he and Calvin Wilkins led a team of 10 Kentucky Baptists to Russia to develop a strategy for the four basic areas of need our partnership agreed to address. As 1994 approached, we made a special effort to create as much exposure as possible for this partnership among both Russian Baptists and Kentucky Baptists. No one would benefit from a timid beginning.

Bold missions work requires bold missions praying. Delores Spears became the partnership's statewide prayer coordinator, enlisting and training prayer coordinators at the association and church levels throughout the state. She also developed a prayer needs communication network to keep partnership concerns before a large and faithful corps of people committed to pray. Their prayers proved to be invaluable, as we saw things happen that could only be attributed to the power of God, invoked by this loyal corps of intercessors.

Even before his election as president of the Russian Baptist Union, Pyotr Konovalchik's deep concern was planting new churches in Russia. He pleaded for this to be a high priority in the new partnership. These churches would need pastors, and the pastors would need financial help for church meeting places as well as for their own basic living expenses.

One of the first requests to Kentucky Baptist churches was for help with the Russian Home Missionary Project. For $200 a month at that time, a church could provide a pastor's salary and living space, and rental for a "house of prayer," a meeting place for a new congregation. Churches, associations, and even individuals responded enthusiastically to this request. Soon, support for more than 100 Russian home missionaries was on the way—most for commitments of 2 years or more.

These new pastors and many others who were already serving churches, most of whom were bivocational, desperately needed and wanted training in order to do their work more effectively. But because of the distance involved and the fact that they could not leave their other jobs, attending the Baptist seminary in Moscow was not an option for most. Joe DeLeon, who with his wife, Gloria, began career missionary service in St. Petersburg in November 1992, quickly realized the need for clergy training and organized schools where pastors could study for minisemesters, taught by experienced faculty who would be recruited from Kentucky and other states.

Volunteer professors came in pairs and taught for a 9-day session that stretched over successive weekends, enabling the pastors to attend the session with only one week away from homes and jobs. It was an exhausting schedule but the results were rewarding. Pastors went home with new knowledge and skills, encouraged in their ministry and with a good feeling about the partnership. Volunteers went home to tell others about the joys of being involved in the partnership.

Every facet of Kentucky Baptist life seemed to reflect a burning desire to see this new work of God off to a good start. In September 1993, Baptist Healthcare System of Kentucky sponsored the first ministry project in the new partnership. They sent a 21-member team of medical, pastoral, and support personnel from five Kentucky Baptist hospitals to minister in Russia for two weeks. The team provided a variety of medical services through clinics set up in a church, the Russian Baptist Union, and several children's hospitals. They treated some 600 people, many of whom had never seen a doctor or dentist. They also distributed hundreds of Bibles and conducted worship services each day.

Some help for the partnership came from unexpected sources. First Baptist Church of Jackson, Mississippi, donated gifts that a Kentucky volunteer team distributed in St. Petersburg at Christmas just as the partnership officially began. The response was rewarding, and Kentucky

Baptist missions organizations across the state donated gifts so that the project could be repeated the next two Christmases in Moscow.

Music is a passion among Russian people. Many with no interest at all in God or His church are attracted to a quality musical presentation, even one in a church. Richard Dwyer, a minister of music in Lexington, Kentucky, had long been interested in Russian culture and had studied the Russian language extensively. With these abilities, he was able to offer valuable assistance in planning and coordinating several excellent music projects that resulted not only in new Christian believers but also in a broader understanding within the churches of the potential of church music for evangelistic outreach.

In May 1994 a 24-member group from the Southern Baptist Theological Seminary in Louisville participated in a 17-day mission to do what music professor Phillip Landgrave called "church music planting." Dividing into five teams, they conducted music workshops and led worship music in churches in outlying areas one week and in Moscow churches the next.

That same month the Georgetown College Chorale took a 30-member team to Moscow and St. Petersburg churches. The trip coincided with a school for interpreters that Robbie and I taught at Central Baptist Church in St. Petersburg. Four of our students were members of the church choir and sang with the Georgetown students at rehearsal on Thursday night and in the worship service on Sunday. An almost instantaneous camaraderie developed as the two cultures merged in songs of praise to God. Each had learned songs in the other's language, and tunes common to both languages enabled them to understand songs whose words they did not recognize.

In a reciprocal arrangement, *Blagovestie* (Good News), the foremost religious folk music ensemble in Russia, toured Kentucky in November 1994. Dressed in colorful Russian dress and playing traditional Russian instruments, these seven talented musicians won the hearts of Baptists across the state and significantly heightened the awareness of this partnership work.

July 1995 brought the partnership's largest missions team. The Kentucky Baptist Chorale and the Kentucky Baptist Singing Women combined to make up a team of 65 members. In addition to numerous concerts, this group spread out to do a variety of other ministries including music training schools and Bible distribution. They participated in baptism services for over 50 converts from three different churches.

Ronald Sholar, minister of music at First Baptist Church in Hazard, Kentucky, returned with warm words of appreciation from a Russian pastor. "Your singing, testimonies, and witnessing have captured the hearts and souls of our Russian people. You will always be with us. We send our warmest thanks and appreciation to your loved ones and the Baptists in Kentucky who sent you. We thank God for you."

Building relationships. Those early projects were designed to do some of that, but no one could have anticipated the depth and breadth of that aspect of the Kentucky-Russia partnership. Following each project, volunteers returned to Kentucky with new friends they will cherish for the rest of their lives, and they left behind people who felt the same about them.

Often initially reserved, Russians quickly accept a sincere offer of friendship and return it with graciousness equal that of any people in the world. Their hospitality is unsurpassed. Russian hosts opened their homes to volunteers so unselfishly as to invite abuse of the offer, but with such a generous spirit that to take advantage of them would have been unthinkable. Many times the Russian people left their homes, giving them over completely to volunteer teams, returning only long enough to prepare meals for their guests. And many more times they prepared sumptuous meals they could only have provided by borrowing food from neighbors and spending money they did not have. As well as we knew how, we tried never to allow such hospitality to go unreimbursed, but they never extended it with that expectation.

Mikhail Pavlovich Petrov—Misha, to use the traditional Russian "short name"—quickly became my friend. Early in our first interpreters school he demonstrated a good grasp of English. When I asked him how he had learned it he surprised me with his answer. "From American music," he said. A fireman by trade, single and living at home, he enjoyed listening to music tapes and was especially fond of the music of Andrew Lloyd Webber. By reading English-language books and listening to English-language music lyrics, he had taught himself our language.

Good-humored and eager to learn, he frequently interrupted Alan and me with questions that provided excellent teaching opportunities. He quickly gained the respect of all the students and became their leader by consensus. He played one of the guitars Alan had brought—again self-taught—and helped to make the classes more enjoyable.

In order to give the interpreters opportunities to practice their skills in a less artificial setting than the classroom, we took them on occasional excursions into Moscow. We toured the Kremlin and explored popular shopping areas on Old Arbat Street, GUM, and Izmailovsky Park.

We traveled the city on the famous Moscow subway, the Metro. The busiest subway in the world, it is a masterpiece of transportation as well as cultural enlightenment. Its older stations, built with forced labor under Stalin's reign, display heroic battle motifs in impressive bronze sculpture, colorful mosaic artworks depicting socialist propaganda messages, and other themes popular during the years of Communism. The interpreters became our tour guides, teaching us about their history and about their fascinating country.

While the other interpreters were sometimes reticent and slow to speak up, Misha always seemed able and willing to explain the meaning of what we saw. Alan and I came to appreciate him more as the class progressed. At the end of the week Misha invited the two of us to visit with him and his family in their home in Kimri, where his father was pastor of the Baptist church. It was an excellent opportunity to experience another facet of Russian culture, so we gladly accepted the invitation. Because the family could not afford a telephone and he had no other way to communicate the news of our visit, Misha left Friday night by train. We agreed to take the morning train and spend Saturday with his family.

It could have been intimidating. Kostya had driven us to the sprawling train station in Moscow, bought our tickets for us, and escorted us to our train car. As the train pulled away from the station, I realized that Alan and I might well be the only ones on the train who spoke English, and the only ones who did not speak Russian. Somehow, though, I felt safe. Even at that early date I was learning that the "Evil Empire" I had heard about for so long was made up of people who were mostly like me—people who meant no harm to others and only wanted to get along in their world.

The *elektrichka* train was surprisingly quiet as it eased up to its travel speed. Ours was not a luxury car, however. The seats were hard benches covered with a yellow vinyl. Heat came from what appeared to be a charcoal burner underneath my seat, but it was not enough to warm more than my back. Age had taken its toll on the car, and the windows fit poorly. A heavy snow blew past my window and leaked around what should have been a weather seal. After a while I noticed that snow was accumulating on the inside of the window. The car was so cold at window height that the snow leaking in did not melt during the entire trip!

In all my life I had not seen a landscape so bleak and desolate looking as that passing outside my window. The heavy cloud cover and the late January morning gave the appearance of never-ending dawn. The birch trees with their white bark flecked with black seemed to melt into the heavy snow that covered everything with a thick, white blanket. Only the top of an occasional barn or silo broke through the whiteness to give evidence of anyone living near where we passed.

Every 30 minutes or so the train stopped at a platform that seemed to appear out of nowhere. At some of the stops passengers exited or boarded the train. Now and then as we slowed for a stop, I looked out the window to see people walking through the snow, coats buttoned up tight, wearing *shapkas*, the traditional fur hats so practical in this Russian winter. Some of them pulled sleds laden with firewood or bundles wrapped against the weather.

Only a few passengers shared our car. They rode in silence, not smiling, seemingly oblivious to anything or anyone around them. A man and woman got on the train together and sat down together but made no conversation. Children sat quietly with mothers, not squirming and fretting at what must have been for them a long and boring ride. Trying not to make anyone uncomfortable, I looked at their faces one by one. Nothing in their expressions betrayed any interest in their surroundings or any anticipation about their destination. What would our welcome be like from this Russian family who did not know us?

Three hours after leaving Moscow we pulled into the station at Kimri, a city of 70,000 people, small by Russian standards. Misha's family had no car, but he had arranged for a friend who did to provide transportation. Alan and I climbed in the back of the small Russian-made car and we started out on the snow-covered street away from the station.

Apparently there had been no attempt to remove snow as it fell, and traffic had compacted it into a thick layer of ice. Only the deep ruts indicated the direction of the streets, and in places they dipped into holes or rose over mounds, making driving rough and hazardous. None of that slowed the driver, however, and as we sped through the treacherous streets, I felt as if I were on some kind of bobsled roller coaster. Still speeding, we crossed the high Volga River bridge. The river was completely frozen over and people were walking across it.

As we came off the bridge Misha asked the driver to stop near the river. We got out of the car and followed

Misha down what looked like it might be a narrow road covered with deep snow. Coming to an open area, we looked out on an impressive view, even though it was all covered in white. It was a large point of land cornering at the frozen confluence of the Kimriki and Volga Rivers. On a high hill across the river stood an old Russian Orthodox Church, dominating the view. The bridge we had crossed, the main traffic artery in and out of the city, looked down on the place where we stood.

This, Misha said, was the site on which they would erect their new church building. The city had given the land to them with the agreement that they would make significant progress on a building within 2 years—something that local governments were doing all over Russia at the time. It was a beautiful location, even covered with snow as it was, and offered excellent visibility to attract the thousands of unchurched people in the city. This would be a wonderful construction opportunity for the partnership!

Most Russians live in high-rise apartment buildings—tall structures clustered together in an incredible sameness of architecture and appearance. Misha's parents lived in one of the single-family homes in Kimri that reflect the older Russia. Behind a pair of white-barked birch trees, the small house sat deep in the snow, enclosed by a neat board fence. It was painted dark green, with a tin roof and the ornate white wood trim so typical of this style of home.

Pastor Pavel Petrov, Misha's father, greeted us warmly. A short man of average build with a full head of black hair, he smiled as he offered a firm handshake and Russian hug to Alan and me. Tamara, his wife, shyly smiled her greeting. Her plain dark clothes and knitted cap were typical peasant style. We removed our boots, as is the custom upon entering a Russian home. Immediately Pastor Pavel announced that we would pray. Standing in the small hallway we all bowed while he voiced a prayer, translated by Misha, thanking God for our safe travel and asking for His blessing as we visited that day.

The train had had no toilet, so I asked Misha for directions to theirs. He showed me to a door near where we had entered the house, and apologized for the lack of facilities. I didn't know what he meant until I opened the door. As a boy growing up in the rural South, I was accustomed to a privy. But I had never seen one indoors! This one was much like those from my childhood, but it was built into a corner of the house. As I thought about it, they had little choice. In the backyard the snow was three feet deep, and it would fall throughout the long winter. This was a very practical location.

Misha then showed me where I could wash my hands. The kitchen sink with only a cold water spigot was the lone source of water in the house. As I washed up, I looked around the small kitchen. Pots steamed on the small gas stove. Two tiny, shriveled carrots lay beside the sink. Preserved vegetables and fruits filled jars placed on scant shelf space. A small, naked lightbulb hung from the ceiling. With a visit to Kimri, pastors in Kentucky who felt underpaid could learn what real poverty is like.

The living room was also small. Russians have a genius for finding storage space, and the glossy-finished, woodgrain cabinets they are so fond of covered one wall. The furnishings were inexpensive and appeared to have been used for a long time—perhaps handed down from church members. Everything was neat and clean. They did well with what they had.

Pastor Pavel wasted no time in showing us their "church." Years before when the congregation needed a place to meet, he had graciously offered his home. Over the years they grew and needed more space. With the congregation unable to build a church, Pastor Pavel personally borrowed money to enlarge his "house of prayer." He escorted us through the modest facility. In the back of the house was a room no larger than an average living room in Kentucky. Furnished with benches for seating, a pulpit, and an old pump organ, it served as the sanctuary. Down a steep stairway was a basement area the same size as the sanctuary, divided into two sparsely furnished classrooms and a small workroom.

This was the Kimri Baptist Church. For more years than most of the members could remember, this was where they had gathered faithfully week after week for worship that sustained them through times of hardship and persecution. During the worst of those times these dedicated Baptists often had to meet discreetly to avoid persecution. Whenever the authorities asked them about their gathering they would say they were having a birthday party. Sometimes it would be a party for one of the members, and sometimes it would be for Jesus!

We talked at length, with Misha interpreting both ways, about the church, Pastor Pavel's work, and their hopes and dreams for the future. They needed a lot of help. As Misha had gone to Moscow for the interpreters school, he had also gone to meet with the architecture consultant for the Russian Baptist Union. It had been a disappointing meeting. Over the years the congregation had saved money from the faithful contributions of its members, looking forward to a time when they would enjoy the freedom they now had to construct a church building. That time had now come, and they had a beautiful location, but skyrocketing inflation in the last 3 years had made their savings worthless. What so recently would have been enough money to build a church building now would not even pay for the architect's work in drawing up the plans.

In spite of this disappointing news, Pastor Pavel was not discouraged. As we moved to the living room, now converted to a dining room by opening a drop-leaf table, he ushered us to our chairs with a good humor developed through long years of depending on God for everything. Tamara had prepared a feast for us. But first we stood for the customary prayer of blessing which Pastor Pavel asked me to offer.

Russians enjoy their mealtimes for the food but even more for the fellowship, especially when they have guests. Tamara served bowls of borscht, the hearty, traditional soup made with cabbage, beets and other vegetables, and we resumed our conversation. Many traditional Russian dishes—sausages, marinated fish, pickled tomatoes and cucumbers—as well as more familiar dishes like potatoes and kraut and cheese, circled the table almost without pause, all accompanied by the delicious black and white breads. We enjoyed beverages of refreshing Russian tea and a sweet fruit compote.

Every time I thought the meal was surely over, Tamara brought out still more dishes. I was feeling stuffed, but I made the mistake of cleaning my plate. Russians find that unacceptable and insist on putting more food on an empty plate. Finally I had to leave food on my plate so that I could stop eating. Then, as we continued the lively conversation, Tamara brought out several delicious desserts, insisting that we try them all. I thought about the bountiful meal she had put before us. It could not have come from this family's meager income. I knew they must have had food brought in from church members and friends, and perhaps spent money earmarked for other needs. But such is the generous hospitality of these gracious people.

After everyone had finished eating we stood for another prayer of blessing, as is the Russian custom. After Tamara had removed the dishes we again sat around the table talking, with Misha faithfully interpreting for all of us. The early morning trip and the heavy meal began to take their toll and my mind strayed. Outside, the subfreezing temperature had formed a beautiful pattern of ice crystal swirls on the windowpanes, and they caught the late afternoon sun in brilliant luminescence. In just such a way, I thought, the warmth of this devoted Christian family illuminated these humble surroundings, creating a radiance that had found a place of contact somewhere deep inside me.

The afternoon turned to evening much too quickly. Our hosts insisted that we stay the night with them, but we were expected back in Moscow and we had to return. Before we could leave, however, Tamara went into a back room and returned with a gift for us. Russians love to give gifts, and she was not to be denied that joy. Our visit came just after Christmas, and Tamara gave us the ornaments from their Christmas tree. They were simple, painted-glass ornaments, probably not expensive, but I have never received a gift that I considered of greater value. They have graced the trees in our home each Christmas since then.

We said our good-byes as Misha's friend waited in the car for us. Misha did not want us to arrive in Moscow unaccompanied and insisted on riding back with us on the train. His fireman's job allowed him free transportation, he assured us, and he would not feel like a good host if he did not do that much.

The train pulled out of the Kimri station through the gathering dusk. A few minutes later it stopped at a platform that stood lonely in the fading light. A middle-aged woman boarded our car and sat down facing me two seats away. Her black overcoat was buttoned up to meet the scarf around her neck. Her fur hat covered her hair. She met my gaze with no change of expression, just the melancholy look I came to expect from these people I wanted so much to understand. Christian believers were proving easy to connect with, but what about these people with whom I did not have that common bond? With the language barrier and their stoic demeanor, how would I be able to reach out to them enough to make a difference?

Kimri Baptist Church

Kimri Baptist Church, built onto the home of pastor Pavel Petrov after the city withdrew its gift of land for a new location.

Kimri Baptist Church members enjoy fellowship after Sunday morning worship

Pastor Pavel Petrov and his wife, Tamara, enjoy their grandchildren outside Kimri Baptist Church

Interpreters school, Moscow, March 1995

5

FAITH TO SHARE

The directions were confusing, and the darkness conspired with the big, fluffy snowflakes to make everything look alike. We tramped through drifted snow a foot deep, taking two wrong turns down the narrow backstreets before finally locating the church. The small, nondescript, concrete block building could easily be overlooked. Only a crudely lettered sign near the entrance identified it, proclaiming in Russian: God Is Love.

We were cold and wet from the snow and eager to get inside. It was exactly 6:30, the time Boris Berezhnoi had told us to arrive, but the church service had already started. I shushed the others as they came in behind me, thumping snow off their boots as I had just done. The people were praying, so we stood in the back of the church, trying not to disturb them.

Second Baptist Church in Moscow was almost full on this Tuesday night, all 50 or so worshipers standing as they prayed. Fervent voices—all women—prayed aloud in Russian, the gentle passion in their voices communicating to me what their words conveyed to God. No sooner did one conclude than another began, with not even a breath of pause between them. I was deeply moved, even though I did not understand anything they said. I envisioned quiet tears in God's eyes as He listened to their petitions.

It had not taken us long to be invited to a Russian worship service. It was Monday of the first interpreters school and we were eating lunch in the dining hall of the Russian Baptist Union. Alexander sat at a table across the room, talking with a Russian I didn't recognize. As we finished eating, Alexander came over to talk with me. His friend was Boris Berezhnoi, the leader of the Russian music group Blagovestie. He was also associate pastor of nearby Second Baptist Church.

Boris invited me to preach at their Tuesday night worship service, and he asked Alan Chamness to sing. We accepted the invitation. Our partnership projects would be generated through Russian churches, and this would be a good opportunity to learn more about them. It would also be good to experience a real Russian service. Our worship the day before had been in the International Baptist Church.

Boris gave Alexander directions to the church. When we returned to class I asked the student interpreters to go with us so that they could see some of what they would be doing.

After a half hour of prayer, a man's voice interrupted the others with a concluding prayer. The man then came to the back of the church to greet us, introducing himself in English. He was Oleg Zhidulov, the senior pastor, and he had learned English as he studied in America. He asked who we were, and why Alan and I were in Russia. As I answered his questions I looked around for Boris, but he was not there. After a bit, I realized that Pastor Oleg was not expecting us. Apparently Boris had neglected to tell him he had invited us.

No matter. Pastor Oleg asked if any of us was a preacher. When the interpreters identified me he said, "You will preach for us." Then he asked if anyone was a singer. When they told him Alan was, he said, "You will sing." We didn't bother to tell him that we had come at Boris's invitation, prepared to do just that. He talked with the interpreters in Russian, making more assignments as I found out later.

By then everyone was looking at us, so Pastor Oleg ushered us to the front of the church and introduced us. We took our seats, with a student between Alan and me to interpret for us. The pastor made announcements and led worship music, playing the piano for accompaniment. Then he called on our students to come to the platform, where they sang a hymn. Tamara, one of the students, recited a beautiful poem about believers being in heaven immediately after their death.

Alan sang; then, it was my turn. As I preached, Tatiana Soboleva interpreted for me. It was my first time to preach through an interpreter in a church setting. I felt awkward at first, pausing after each short sentence while Tatiana repeated it in Russian. I wondered if I was communicating at all. When I finished, Tatiana interpreted my last sentence, and added, "Amen." I learned another Russian custom.

Pastor Oleg then requested that we allow the congregation to ask us questions. With Tatiana interpreting, Alan and I answered questions for half an hour. Another time of prayer followed this, and the congregation shared concerns that Tatiana interpreted for us. One woman kept orphans in her home and asked for prayer for them. Another wanted prayer for young people who faced so many temptations.

After this lengthy prayer session, Pastor Oleg concluded the service—more than 2 hours after we had arrived! And no one was in any hurry to leave even then! If this was typical Russian worship, I wondered who would be helping whom in this partnership. Many Kentucky Baptists would feel the need to catch up with these Russian Baptists.

The passion Russian Baptists demonstrate in their worship is equaled by their passion to see their countrymen become Christians. But most of them have a lot to learn when it comes to outreach. Under the Communists, Christian believers were forbidden to evangelize, even among their own families. According to their accounts, parents sometimes were imprisoned when their children reported such activity to the KGB. Now, for this generation of believers, sharing their faith was a new concept requiring skills they would need to learn.

But there was no lack of opportunity. Unbelievers regularly attend services in Russian Baptist churches. Often a spouse's or parent's walk of faith attracts unbelieving family members. Some who were formerly active in the Communist party are now drawn to God and His church through the deep faith they see in people whom they persecuted and harassed. Often one of the millions of Russian alcoholics reaches out in desperation for deliverance from a horrible addiction.

For these and others, however, the greatest attraction seemed to us to be that God was moving in some mysterious way in Russia, and He was doing it through these churches so long repressed. The Russian people were somehow coming to realize that as Communism with its utopian promises had failed miserably, God's church was still alive and vibrant after all the years of persecution. Maybe *this* was the better way, *the* way to survive when your world seemed about to collapse around you.

Yevgeniy Samsonyenko was proof of that.

Our second interpreters school took place in Moscow in May 1994. We were in a different location this time, a hotel initially built to house athletes for the 1980 Summer Olympics, the ones boycotted by the United States. The hotel was not far from Sheremetyevo Airport, in a pleasant setting with views of open fields and modest houses. Thick groves of birch trees behind and to one side invited quiet strolls around the grounds.

Other guests also occupied the hotel, some attending conferences, but most appearing to be vacationers. Their noisy parties lasted into the early morning hours, and we never saw them until late in the day. Our class schedule kept us separated except at mealtimes.

The dining room had not opened when we broke for lunch that day. As Larry Lindsey and I talked, I noticed an old man across the lobby. I had seen him the day before in the same place. Slightly built, he had thin white hair atop a weathered face with a stubbly, gray beard. His clothes, neither shabby nor expensive, consisted of the usual drab-colored pants and shoes topped with a clean shirt and a rumpled wool suit coat. His leathery hands and stooped back indicated that he had worked hard during his long life. He had been watching us for several minutes.

Slowly he began to move in our direction. He seemed to be trying to hear our conversation. As he came near, a slight smile broke across his face. "Amerikanski, da?" he asked.

When I answered, "Da," he offered his hand to shake mine, gripping it warmly with both hands as his smile seemed to cover his face. He greeted Larry the same way.

"Yevgeniy Samsonyenko," he said by way of introduction. We told him our names in response. He spoke only a few words of English, and we knew even less Russian, but we began to piece together a fascinating conversation.

"I believer," he volunteered immediately, although the conversation Larry and I were having when he approached included nothing that indicated we were Christians.

We told him we were believers also, and that we were Baptist. His face brightened even more. "I Baptist!" he exclaimed, and shook our hands again, even more warmly this time.

Alexander noticed our gathering and came over to interpret for us. The old man was a guest at the hotel. His wife, a patient in a nearby Moscow hospital, was being treated for a serious heart condition. As soon as her condition stabilized, they would fly to New York, where their son lived. He had arranged for his mother to have open-heart surgery. Yevgeniy asked if we would pray for his wife.

We bowed where we were and joined arms for the prayer. I prayed for both of them, thanking God for the privilege of meeting a new brother in Christ. I prayed that his wife's condition would stabilize so that they could make the trip and for their safe travel and her successful surgery. Larry continued the prayer, asking God's blessing on these two who had served Him faithfully in difficult times.

As we said our amens, I saw tears in the old man's eyes. He grinned broadly and thanked us repeatedly. Then he caught me completely by surprise as he grabbed me in a strong embrace and kissed me full on the lips. That was a first for me, and I felt awkward and embarrassed. But I knew this was a Russian tradition and I accepted it with the Christian brotherly love I knew it expressed.

Then he surprised me again. He reached inside his coat and brought out something wrapped in a clear plastic bag. Handing it to me he said, "Gift for you."

I opened the bag to find a beautiful, hand-carved wooden chain. He had made it himself. From a single piece of birch log, he had carved connecting links to form a 2-foot-long chain, polishing it by hand to a velvety smooth finish. He explained that the hospital only allowed a brief visit with his wife each day, and this was the way he passed the rest of his time at the hotel. He told Larry he had another chain in his room and promised to bring it to him.

By now Robbie, Joy Lindsey, and the other interpreters had gathered around and were also enjoying the visit. It was a family reunion for all of us. The hotel opened the dining room, and I invited him to join us for lunch. I wanted to know more about this fascinating old man, and he was more than willing to oblige.

The horrors of World War II were the pivotal point in Yevgeniy Samsonyenko's history. Fresh out of high school, he was called up to fight the Germans who were invading Russia. A miracle, he said, had saved him from almost certain death, and he found a connection between that event and his new friends from Kentucky.

As a way to teach the interpreters about Kentucky, Robbie and I had brought souvenir lapel pins with the silhouette of a thoroughbred horse. Yevgeniy noticed the one on Alexander's coat, and it reminded him of a time long ago.

Just out of infantry boot camp, he was assigned to go with thousands of other soldiers to what was then Leningrad, now St. Petersburg, to face the German army. The Russian soldiers were poorly trained and poorly equipped, and he knew that most of them never came back home. As his unit was loaded onto a troop train to make the trip north, he thought he was seeing Moscow for the last time.

Somewhere in the Tver region the train made a stop. An army officer in charge of some horses asked if anyone on board knew how to care for them. Yevgeniy had learned about horses as a boy and volunteered the information to the officer. He was taken off the train and reassigned to care for the horses, spending the rest of the war safely out of the fighting. Knowing about horses, he said, had saved his life.

In colorful and dramatic detail the old man told us story after animated story. He had been a believer during the terrible Communist years, and life had been incredibly difficult. Maybe his wife's illness would bring some well-deserved blessing in their later years. His son had a home for them to live in when they got to America. In any case, there were blessings in store for them. The Father also had prepared a home for them.

World War II proved to be an excellent point of connection for us with the Russians, especially older men who were otherwise hard to reach. In spite of the cold war, Russian veterans and others remembered that our countries were allies against Hitler's armies. They credit American troops with saving their nation from much greater devastation than it experienced, possibly even from defeat. Many times during our partnership Russian veterans presented their war medals as gifts to Kentucky veterans.

We constantly looked for ways to connect with these people from such a different culture. Gardening proved to be another effective way. With so many Russians unemployed, and as many or more not getting paid for their work, kitchen gardens are a major source of food for many families. In the spring, many families board buses and even the Metro with seed potatoes and gardening tools and head out of the cities to tend their small but precious garden plots. Some who can afford larger plots spend weeks at a time there, enjoying a respite from the city in their *dachas*, which can be anything from a small hut to a large, multistory summer home. The Russians enjoyed garden talk with their Kentucky guests, and on occasion took them out for a visit to their plots.

Kentucky volunteers from every walk of life invariably met Russian counterparts with whom they could find much in common. These connections helped build deep and lasting friendships and often provided windows of opportunity for volunteers to share their faith in Christ. The Russians were hungry for the good news.

"Now is the time for the gospel in Russia." That was the vision of Vladimir Boyev as the Kentucky-Russia partnership began. And he has the background to make that judgment. Reared in an orphanage because his parents could not care for him, he became a street hoodlum as a teenager. He fell in love with and married the daughter of a Baptist pastor, and the church in turn loved him into faith in Christ.

Life for Boyev was good after that, but it was far from easy. God turned his dynamic personality toward a ministry. Both his father and father-in-law were murdered because of their faith, and the KGB destroyed Boyev's church and tried unsuccessfully to have him killed. He endured years of harassment because of his work with Russian Baptists.

When the partnership began between Russian and Kentucky Baptists, Boyev was director of home missions for the Russian Baptist Union. He presented a bold challenge to Baptists on both sides of the partnership: Begin 1,000 new congregations in the new Russia. That was the spark for the Russian Home Missionary Project, and he worked hard to fan it into flame.

In early 1995, the small Baptist congregation in Yelets, 250 miles south of Moscow, needed a church building. This group of 25 members was the only evangelical church in a city of 140,000 people, and Vladimir Boyev believed there was far more potential there. For $15,000 they could buy an existing building that would be suitable for the church. He presented the need to Kentucky Baptists.

Members of Binghamtown Baptist Church in Middlesboro donated the entire amount. When the money reached Moscow, Larry Lindsey and Norman Lytle caught the train to Yelets to deliver it. The pastor and Vladimir Boyev met them at the train station in Yelets and drove them to the converted chicken house where the church met. It was a cold and snowy Saturday morning in January, and there was no heat in the building. Nevertheless, some 60 people were jammed inside, waiting to begin a service of praise to God for providing the money for their building.

With Vladimir interpreting, Larry and Norman preached. Then the pastor preached a third sermon. Because of impending bad weather, Larry and Norman needed to hurry back to the train station. A major snowstorm was approaching and the road there would be impassable if the storm hit before they got there. The pastor closed the service without extending an invitation to commitment so that the two men could be on their way.

As they were leaving the church, two young men arrived and approached Larry. Both were 19-year-old students at the technical institute in Yelets. They had heard that two Americans were coming who could tell them Who God is, and they asked Larry if he would tell them. Larry shared the gospel with them and asked the first one if he would like to pray to receive Christ as his personal Savior. He knelt with Larry, repented, and believed. Larry repeated the question to the second young man and he did the same. In Larry's words, "I praised God and looked at my watch."

Again they started to leave, and again they were stopped, this time by a middle-aged couple. They too wanted to hear about Jesus, and again Larry shared the gospel. Both of them knelt, prayed, and became Christians. Only later did Larry and Norman learn that these two were the owners of the building the church was buying, and they had only come to the service to receive payment for the building. Now they had learned how their sins had been paid for as well!

But the day was far from over. By now Larry and Norman were beginning to feel panic as they thought about the drive to the station and the approaching storm. Again they were stopped, this time by a woman with an urgent request. Her husband, retired from the Russian army, had been assigned retirement quarters in a nearby village. Because she was the only believer there, she often came to Yelets to worship, as she had that day. She wanted Larry and Norman to come to her village and hold a worship service.

They decided to trust God to care for them in the snowstorm and agreed to go with the woman. Some of the church members from Yelets accompanied them. In spite of whiteout conditions on the way, they made the 12-mile drive from Yelets. She directed them to a cultural hall, again unheated. The temperature outside was well below freezing, and that inside was not much better.

While Larry and Norman waited, the woman and the members from Yelets spread the word that Americans were there to hold a worship service. Soon a crowd of about 85 people had gathered. The woman who owned the cultural hall stood in the doorway watching.

Some of the church members from Yelets sang. Then both Norman and Larry preached, with Vladimir interpreting. Vladimir gave an invitation after the sermons, and every person there came forward to repent, including the owner of the cultural hall! Together they prayed to receive Christ.

After the service, the woman who had asked for the service announced that she would host a Bible study in her home on Friday nights. She invited everyone in the village to attend. The next week the Yelets Baptist Church began a regular Friday night Bible study in her home with the pastor or a deacon coming to lead it.

The much-anticipated snowstorm was delayed far beyond the time it had been predicted, and Larry and Norman arrived at the station in time for their return train to Moscow. Both men remain in awe of what God did on that glorious Saturday in January. How hungry the Russians were to hear the gospel!

The Metro car was crowded when we boarded it in the heart of Moscow, but at each stop along the route to the edge of the city it emptied a few more passengers. Our group had scattered as we boarded, taking whatever seats were available. I sat alone, studying the expressionless faces of the remaining passengers across from me.

Voracious readers that they are, Russians often hide behind books, magazines, and newspapers while riding the Metro. Some of my fellow passengers did that. Others without reading material stared blankly, refusing to allow me even a return glance. I wondered if there was a way to approach them and share the gospel in such an environment as that with any hope of a positive response.

Robbie was doing much better than I. She and Natasha Alyekina, a university student from Smolensk, were deep in conversation. Natasha had come to the interpreters school at the prompting of Kinney Mitchell, a missionary in her city. She was a member of the Russian Orthodox Church, but she attended a Bible study that Kinney and his wife, Elise, taught each week. Feeling that the exposure to a group of Baptists would be good for her, they had made the arrangements for her to attend the school.

Natasha's English was very good, and she had a real talent for interpreting. But her questions during the week had indicated the likelihood of some internal conflict between her Orthodox background and the Baptist theology we often discussed. She and Robbie had become good friends; and now as they sat together at the other end of the car, she asked Robbie what it meant to her to be a Christian believer.

Robbie answered her question and asked her if they might move up the car to include me in the conversation. For the remainder of our trip the three of us talked about the significant differences between the two faiths. We focused primarily on the personal and direct relationship to Christ to which Baptists cling, and how becoming a believer is a miracle of God that comes through faith in Christ alone, without the need for anyone or any church as a mediator.

Seeing her struggle with this new concept, I knew she was genuinely seeking God's direction. We had other opportunities to talk about these things as the school went on, but she never reached the point of making a commitment. Before Natasha left to return home, Robbie and I prayed with her and asked her to keep in touch.

The next week we were in St. Petersburg for another school. As we returned one afternoon to the apartment where we were staying, the phone rang. It was Natasha, calling from Smolensk to tell us that she had accepted Christ and had shared her decision in the Baptist church in Smolensk the previous Sunday.

That was in 1994. Natasha finished her degree in English the next year and then came to Grand Rapids, Michigan, where she studied at Reformed Theological Seminary. Today she is back in Russia, serving as a missionary in St. Petersburg. Her letters to us reflect a vibrant and growing faith as she shares the gospel with her fellow Russians. She has also written to tell us that she has led her younger brother to faith in Christ. Her parents, not yet believers, now allow her to pray at mealtimes when she visits them, and they are willing to discuss matters of faith with her when she brings up the subject.

Hundreds of partnership volunteers found the Russians they encountered eager to learn about Christ and His promise of salvation. Sometimes their decisions came slowly, often long after the volunteers had returned home. But once they committed their lives to Christ, they were usually eager to become witnesses themselves. Only heaven will reveal how these commitments were repeated in the lives of others the volunteers never met.

And for many volunteers these experiences of sharing their faith in Russia were their first ever attempts to do so. Thrown into situations where theirs would be the only witness someone would hear, they were empowered by the Holy Spirit to deliver. Often in their postmission evaluations they thanked us for helping them to learn that they could do this. What blessings God provided to those on both sides of this partnership!

But there were many obstacles. Satan saw to that.

Kentucky partnership coordinators Nancy and Bob Walden with Misha Petrov outside Second Baptist Church in Moscow. This is the first Baptist church building completed in Moscow in over 100 years. It was dedicated October 25, 1998.

6

HIS GRACE IS SUFFICIENT

It was almost midnight when we boarded the train, Robbie and I sharing a four-person compartment with Tatiana Soboleva. Having just completed an interpreters school in Moscow, we were on our way to St. Petersburg for another. We were looking forward to getting acquainted with Russia's second largest city, forged through a fascinating history.

Peter the Great had been so impressed with the great cities of Europe that he wanted Russian cities to become more like them. He founded St. Petersburg on the Gulf of Finland as Russia's "window on the West" in 1703. Since London had St. Paul's Church, and Rome had St. Peter's, he decided to build a church named for both of these saints (Peter and Paul Cathedral) as the centerpiece of the original fortress. With Peter's support the city became Russia's intellectual and social center, and remains so to this day.

From 1712 to 1917 St. Petersburg was the nation's capital. In 1924 it was renamed Leningrad (Lenin's City) the day after Lenin's death. In one of the most heroic stories of World War II, the Germans laid siege to the city for 900 days. Almost 1 million people died, most of them from starvation, but the city did not fall.

The Hermitage Museum, formerly the Winter Palace of the czars, is located in the heart of this beautiful city. It is Russia's cultural and artistic showpiece par excellence. In 1991 the city renounced its Communist name and once again became St. Petersburg.

As the train rolled out of Moscow, we made the beds in our sleeping car, hoping to get some sleep before our 7:00 A.M. arrival. The rocking of the train and the rhythm of the tracks were soothing, but this was a new experience for Robbie and me, and we found it hard to get to sleep. We had barely dozed off when the train made the first of many stops during the night. At two or three of the stops I awoke to what sounded like someone banging on the undercarriage of the train with a sledgehammer.

The night would have been short enough without any of that. It was mid-May and we were near the season of "white nights" when it never gets completely dark in that far northern part of Russia. Long before we arrived at our destination, I gave up on sleep and stood in the passageway outside the compartment, watching the countryside go by in the dim light of early morning.

Lee and Sarah Bivins, our hosts for that two weeks in St. Petersburg, met us at the station as the train pulled in on schedule. They would be attending a missionary meeting in Moscow for over a week and had given us the use of their apartment while they were away. Joe DeLeon and his assistant, Oleg, also met us at the station and drove us all to Lee and Sarah's apartment building before leaving on other business.

I was tired and sleepy, but thankful to be "home" after the train trip. But we weren't there yet. Apologizing, Lee and Sarah explained that the elevator was out of order, so we had to carry our luggage up nine flights of stairs!

Their apartment was nice and comfortable, and we unpacked and settled into their guest bedroom. A large window looked out on another identical apartment building across an open area. The day was overcast, but the window let in enough light to brighten things up. We would soon realize that the white nights kept things bright around the clock. The sun actually dipped below the horizon, but the entire night never got so dark that we could not read by the light coming in the window. Bedtime seemed never to come, and when we did go to bed, it was like trying to sleep in the daytime.

As soon as we were settled, Lee wanted to run some errands and invited me to go with him. Needing to exchange some money, I went along. The Bivinses had no vehicle at the time, so Lee and I walked. Other apartment buildings surrounded theirs as far as I could see in every direction. Many of them had shops, businesses, and government offices on the ground floors. Besides the bank, we needed to go to the post office, pay utility bills, and pick up a few groceries. That shouldn't take long, I thought. But this was Russia!

First we went to exchange money. At just after noon, many of the shops and offices were closed for their midday break. So was the first bank we tried. And the second. Another couldn't make the exchange. Finally we found a place where we could exchange money, but only one of us could go in at the time. The post office posed little problem. Lee and Sarah had their own box; they just had to make sure to go during the hours it was open. The utility office was open, but the customer line was long, and we had to wait almost 15 minutes before Lee could make his payment.

The grocery store was quite an experience. All of the items were behind counters. Meat and fruits and vegetables were displayed, but not for picking up and taking to a cashier. First Lee chose an item, and then he stood in line to tell the attendant what he wanted. Next he went to a cashier across the store and stood in another line to pay for it. Then he took his receipt and went back to the attendant and stood in line again to get his purchase. He repeated this process for each item he bought.

We had to go to another shop to buy bread, and Lee followed the same procedure there. In all, our stops covered an area of four to six large city blocks. We must have walked at least 2 miles by the time we got back to the apartment. Not all the items Lee wanted were available. For some he was able to substitute and for others he did without.

Sarah prepared a delicious dinner for us, adjusting her menu to what had been available from the market. The day, as well as the night before it, had been long. More than anything, I felt like going to bed after dinner. But the Georgetown College Choir, on tour from Kentucky, was performing at Central Baptist Church that night, and we didn't want to miss them.

Lee opted not to go, so Sarah escorted us to the church, a mile-and-a-half walk in a pouring rain. We could have taken the bus part of the way, but then we would have had to wait in the rain for it to come by. Our rain gear protected us somewhat, but the walk was miserable just the same.

The service turned out to be only a rehearsal. The choir would perform on Sunday. After 2 hours and nice visits with several of the students, we headed back to the apartment, walking all the way in rain pouring just as hard as it had been on our earlier trip. I was even more miserable by the time we got home.

Such is life in Russia. Some of the obstacles change from day to day, but there are always obstacles. Things are never easy. And sometimes the obstacles are much more than minor inconveniences.

The lights from the engine pushed back the darkness as the train rounded the curve and slowed to a stop. Misha Petrov and I stood on the platform outside the railway station in Oryol, waiting to board the train for the trip back to Moscow. It was a trip I had not counted on, and one I felt sick about having to make. The last 36 hours had been agonizing.

Everything had gone well until Sunday. Our flight to Moscow was uneventful, and our accommodations at the Izmailova Hotel were adequate. Sight-seeing and shopping on Friday had also been enjoyable. This was my fifth trip to Russia, so I was content to help the others make the most of that time.

On Saturday our team of volunteers boarded a bus for Oryol, 7 hours south of Moscow. Our project there involved helping construct a new church building, conducting Vacation Bible School, and leading evangelistic services. It was an ambitious project, but we had a capable team and I felt good about what we would be doing.

The European-style tour bus was comfortable, and the box lunches we brought from the hotel were tasty. We laughed about the "rest area" as we stopped beside the highway near the midpoint of the trip. "Guys to the left and girls to the right," someone said as we waded through tall weeds to get to the woods.

As we came into the city, a car pulled onto the road and passed the bus, the driver and a passenger waving to us. Some of the volunteers had been to Oryol the previous year and recognized them as the pastor and a deacon from the church. They escorted us to the new church building, a striking white brick structure, modern in its architecture and highly visible from the main highway into the city.

The building was under a roof but some of the windows were not in, and other than pouring the concrete for the main-floor sanctuary, little had been done inside. In a basement area with only packed earth for a floor, church members had set up long makeshift tables and benches. Thirty or 40 of these fellow believers had gathered and prepared a bountiful meal to welcome us. The rest of the evening was for relaxing and settling in with our host families. Misha and I were guests of a very nice family, a couple in their late 30s with a 14-year-old son.

My only responsibility the next day was preaching in the morning worship service. On Monday we would begin the other facets of the project. Kenny Samples from Mayfield was in charge of the construction, and several women had volunteered to lead Vacation Bible School during part of each day. We would have worship services each night, but two other pastors on the trip would share the preaching responsibilities with me. I was looking forward to a project where I didn't have to make it all happen.

On Sunday morning, the cultural hall was packed for the morning worship service. I had finished preaching and, with no interpretation of the Russian pastor's sermon, my mind wandered to things we would do the next day. All of us had to remember to give our passports and visas to the pastor, who would take them to the local police station to register them, as required by Russian law. Everyone staying three days or more in a location must make that known to the local authorities.

My passport. I hadn't used it since we had checked into the hotel on Thursday. It was in my security pouch, wasn't it? Of course. That's where I always kept it. As soon as the service was over, I found a private place and checked, but it *wasn't* there. I searched my other pockets. Well, it must be back in my room in the clothes I had worn the day before, or in my luggage.

I would never learn what happened to my documents. I searched through everything I had brought. I questioned the others to be sure someone wasn't playing a practical joke on me. Finally, convinced that my important documents were gone, I called Larry and Joy Lindsey back in Moscow. The only other place I could think to look was the tour bus, where they might have fallen out of the saddlebag pocket of my pants. It would be Monday before the Lindseys could inquire about that. In the meantime, they assured me that they would find out about the procedure for replacing my documents. The prospects were grim. They had been told that it would take as much as two weeks for the visa, which would require delaying my return home and rescheduling my flight.

That night I slept little. The next day I could only wait to hear from the Lindseys, so I went on to the church to help out with the project. I spent the day in "brick therapy"—moving oversized white Russian bricks from one pile to another. The tiring physical activity helped, but I couldn't stop thinking about my dilemma.

The only conclusion I could come to was that someone had picked my pocket. When my passport, with my visa inside, was returned to me at the hotel the morning after we arrived, I was jet-lagged and tired. Because I was carrying money for another church in the area, I had chosen an underarm security pouch that was hard to get into. As we left to go sight-seeing, I may have put the documents in the saddlebag side pocket of my pants.

During the day we had ridden a Metro car so crowded that I had to stand, with other people seated and standing all pressed against me. Later as we returned to the hotel, we took a shortcut through an open-air market outside the Metro station. An old woman had stopped me there, talking rapidly and trying to show me something in a book she held. When I tried to go around her, she moved to keep me where I was. That, I finally decided, was the most likely explanation. And that meant I would never see those documents again.

A search of the tour bus was fruitless. From Joy's inquiries she had determined that I would have to return to Moscow immediately to begin the process of replacing my papers. Misha would return with me on the overnight train to be my interpreter. Not only would I miss being part of an important project, I was also taking a valuable interpreter away from the project. And instead of being there to help, I needed help from a lot of other people. It was a miserable prospect. God could have intervened in this situation. Why hadn't He?

Time after time throughout our partnership, we encountered unexpected difficulties we could attribute to nothing other than the work of Satan. Well-laid plans had to be drastically changed. Entire projects had to be canceled or diverted to other locations. Bureaucratic delays were commonplace. Larry Lindsey often told volunteers to watch out for TINA, his acronym for "This Is Not America."

The truth is, Satan is always present where people are doing God's work, in Russia or America or anywhere else. Perhaps it was because God was doing such a marvelous work in so many places in Russia that we saw so much evidence of Satan's activity.

Kimri was a prime example. In the spring of 1994 the winter snow melted, and the leaves and wildflowers emerged on the beautiful building site for the new Kimri Baptist Church. But other things were developing that were ugly and evil. The Russian Orthodox Church in Kimri felt threatened by the prospect of a beautiful new Baptist church in such a prime location. With their considerable political clout, they persuaded the local authorities that they had a prior claim to the site, and the city withdrew its gift to the Kimri Baptist Church. The decision was heartbreaking, but it was irrevocable. The people had a dream, but no land on which to build it.

The Russian bureaucracy was an ever-present force to be reckoned with. Centuries of hand-holding with the Russian Orthodox Church had created a legacy that often meant headaches and heartaches for Russian Baptists, as well as their friends from Kentucky. Each year of the partnership brought increasing delays and escalating costs for issuing visas to volunteers. Banks in Moscow discontinued accepting wire transfers of money for missions projects. And the list goes on and on. The worst of it was that, all the while, our volunteers sought only to give to the people of Russia, never wanting to take from them.

But as often as Satan's efforts created problems, God's power prevailed. Kentucky Baptists learned along with their Russian Baptist friends to look for opportunity in adversity. Sometimes the good that resulted turned out to be greater than what was originally planned. And the strengthened faith of those involved always glorified God.

Getting a new passport proved to be a matter of less than 2 hours. Misha and I were waiting when the American embassy in Moscow opened that Tuesday morning. The personnel there amazed me with their helpfulness and efficiency. By 11:00 A.M., we were on our way to the police station near the Izmailova Hotel to report what I had determined must have been a pickpocketing incident.

Replacing my visa required dealing with the Russian authorities, and that was a different experience altogether. But Misha's help proved to be extremely valuable. At each stop, he explained my situation with a firmness that the Russians understand, never submitting to the intimidation that is so characteristic of their bureaucracy.

After an hour's wait in the police station, we were told that the person in charge was gone to lunch. We could return at 3:00 P.M. With 2 hours to kill, we ate lunch and decided to go to the hotel nearby and search the room where I had stayed. We had no luck, but it felt good to be doing something. We returned to the police station early and were able to go right in and report the incident. The two policemen were courteous and gave me a report to use with my visa application. They also accepted Russian New Testaments that I offered, including one each in picture-book format for their children.

Next it was off to the Russian Baptist Union for a letter from them, as the issuers of my original letter of invitation to Russia. They quickly accommodated us and gave us directions to the government office that issues visas. We arrived too late to get the visa issued that day, and we learned they would be closed the next day, but they promised to have it by Thursday afternoon, which they did. Things were looking much better.

As it turned out, after all the inconvenience and anxiety was behind me, that trip became one of the best I ever made to Russia. In April 1996 I had become associate director of partnership missions for the Kentucky Baptist Convention. Heart bypass surgery three months earlier had made going to Russia inadvisable for me that year. There was much that I still needed to see firsthand in order to have a better understanding of our work. The Lindseys helped me work out an alternate itinerary that enabled me to visit over a dozen churches where we had done projects. I was able to meet many people who had only been names in reports until then. God had turned a difficult situation into a glorious opportunity.

One place I most wanted to visit that week was Kimri. In the 3 years since I had been there, the church had done a major building project with the help of Kentucky volunteers. After they were denied the gift of land from the city, Pastor Pavel graciously offered to allow the church to build on the site where his house stood. Misha was proud of all that his father had done, but concerned that the stress of it all had begun to take its toll on his health. He was eager for me to visit his parents again and to see the new church building. Misha had married shortly before the interpreters school in 1995, and I had met his wife, Natasha, then. They now had a son whom he also wanted me to meet.

It was a delightful visit. I spent two days with Misha and his family. Their son Stepan was 2 years old and learning to talk, but not English! As the four of us sat at the table, I was talking with Misha when Stepan interrupted. "Nyet!" he exclaimed, pointing his finger at me with a reproachful look. He said something else in Russian that I didn't understand, and Misha and Natasha laughed. "Don't look at Papa and speak!" he had said, upset that he couldn't understand the conversation. Before long, however, we were getting along very well. He awakened me each morning calling, "Dyeda Ken" (Grandpa Ken).

Renewing my friendship with Misha's parents was equally enjoyable. Pastor Pavel and I are the same age, and both of us have been pastors for most of our lives. He listened patiently as I encouraged him to pace himself in his work, taking some rest now and then in order to have more years of productive work. From my own experience I warned him what too much stress could do. He objected good-naturedly to some of my suggestions, but his family supported my argument. It was a good visit with a brother I had come to love very much, and I felt that he just might take some of my advice.

Sunday was the icing on the cake. The new Kimri Baptist Church building was beautiful, situated to take maximum advantage of the lot. It included a nice apartment for Pastor Pavel and Tamara, with a modern toilet! A metal tank that served as a baptistry had been brought inside and installed in the basement floor, with a removable cover to make more use of the space. The sanctuary walls and ceiling were beautifully covered with birch planking and plaster, and large windows let in generous quantities of sunlight.

The church was full, as was my heart, as I preached in the morning worship service. The memories of that first visit outside Moscow, the history of this loving couple's sacrifice over the years, and the demonstration of what God can do when people are committed to Him all were overwhelming. God does work in all things for good for those who love Him and are called according to His purpose.

Even with the minor inconveniences. That first trip to St. Petersburg had been tiring, especially the first day. The frustration of spending so much time just to run a few errands. The miserable walk to the church on a Thursday night in the pouring rain. Things were never easy in Russia. But who was I to complain? I would only be there for a short time. The people with whom I worked lived with such things their entire lives. They had a right to complain.

But they didn't. Instead they celebrated Easter! It was May, but Easter is a monthlong celebration in the Russian Baptist church. It is as if a day or even a Holy Week isn't enough time to affirm the Resurrection of Christ and His victory over the worst that Satan can do.

Robbie and I walked to church again on Sunday morning with Lee and Sarah. It was a glorious time. The church was packed. The huge choir loft was filled with Russians and Georgetown College students. The music was heavenly. The spirit of worship was joyous and uplifting. And stretched over the pulpit area in front of a cross-shaped window was the message that said it all. Huge illuminated letters suspended from the ceiling read, *Christus Voskres!* (Christ Is Risen!)

A Kentuckian employs his cabinetmaking skills to help a Russian carpenter build window frames for Transfiguration Baptist Church in Oryol, 1997

Kentuckians and Russians working together outside Transfiguration Baptist Church

Above and below: Construction work on Transfiguration Baptist Church.

Monument to Czar Nicholas I in St. Isaac's Square, St. Petersburg

7

THE RUSSIAN WAY

"*Grusovik.*" For the fifth or sixth time, at least, Misha patiently and slowly pronounced the Russian word for "truck" as the huge Finnish double-trailer rig came into view over the hill. We had driven most of the day and were on the last stretch of highway between St. Petersburg and Vyborg. The road, built to accommodate the heavy truck traffic between Finland and Russia, was wide and well maintained and didn't require the driver's absolute attention. With little to break the monotony of long miles of birch forest, we began to pass the time learning new words in each other's language.

Misha Sokolov was good company. A valued assistant to Lee and Sarah Bivins while they coordinated the partnership work with the churches in the St. Petersburg region, he had a relaxed, unassuming manner that endeared him to the hundreds of volunteers he drove to and from project sites. Many times his down-to-earth wisdom provided solutions for difficult problems that so often stemmed from nothing more than differences between Russian and American cultures.

But he didn't have an answer for the question that kept coming back to haunt me on the long drive home after our visit to Kolpino. "Why do Russian Baptists build churches the way they do?" Wherever we had worked on a new church building it had always been the same. Kolpino was just the most recent example.

It was an incredible sight! So many people! Across the street, as far as the eye could see in either direction, high-rise apartment buildings reached toward the drizzling rain-clouds. Ten thousand, perhaps 20,000, people lived in just the buildings I could see from atop the structure that would be the Kolpino Baptist Church, none more than three or four blocks away. And how many thousands more lived in other apartments just beyond those, still within easy walking distance? I could not recall ever seeing a church site with more potential for reaching people.

Yet right under my feet was a problem that frustrated my practical nature to no end. The wall on which I stood was five bricks thick. And these were no ordinary bricks. They were almost twice the size of standard American bricks. To make matters worse, only mortar filled the spaces between them. Here at the edge of the Arctic Circle there was no insulation to keep out the harsh winter cold. Sections of the wall were enlarged to support the awkward structure, wasting valuable space. Rain dripped through holes in the floors of crudely poured concrete, promising maintenance needs even before construction was completed.

Why, with an economy in shambles and money in such incredibly short supply, did they build this way? Such clumsy architecture made a building like this cost four to five times as much for its usable space as it should have. And heating and maintenance costs could easily double that in a few years.

Besides all that, the building would not be large enough. Just two days earlier the church had held its first worship service on the new site, even without a roof on the building. Brick-and-board benches served as seats, and people filled what would be the sanctuary space. Why not design a larger, more cost-effective building and have room to accommodate more people?

The styles of architecture vary widely in these new Russian churches. The church at Kolpino, now complete, is very gothic in appearance. Multiple sharp steeples outline the metal roof, pointed arches encase tall windows, and elaborate details in the outside brickwork reflect an old style common in many places in Europe. In contrast, the Vyborg church features a very contemporary design. Sitting high on a hill overlooking the Gulf of Finland, it boasts a broad, sweeping galvanized metal roof on one side that rises 4 stories high, like the sail of a huge Viking ship poised to catch the winds blowing in from the ocean. Skylights bring sunlight streaming down into the sanctuary from 50 feet above.

Regardless of the design, however, many common structural details seem archaic and wastefully expensive. I posed these questions to Vasily Byelov, building consultant for the Russian Baptist Union. A professional architect, Byelov was honored for his work by the Soviet Union in 1988. Working for the government until 1990, he designed theaters, sports facilities, and industrial buildings. He is a Baptist, and with the fall of Communism and the opportunity for churches to build, he felt called to bring his talents to work with his brothers and sisters in Christ. He left his government position to become a missionary architect, supported by Kentucky Baptists as part of the Russian Home Missionary Project. Today he travels across Russia, advising churches on construction, designing buildings, and helping pastors properly execute construction documents to satisfy the many levels of Russian bureaucracy.

"Russian Baptists have no architectural style," he explained. "They went so long without being able to construct buildings. Beginning in 1985, new churches were allowed to register with the government, and in 1990, they were allowed to begin new buildings. So they began by simply copying older styles. The new buildings you see today reflect that older way of building."

When I asked about the choice of building materials, Byelov explained that before 1990 only brick was readily available. It was also cheap at that time—$3 for 1,000 bricks. In 1998 the cost for the same quantity had risen to $150, but by then they had already started the buildings. Plaster and insulation were not available; or if they were, they were inferior materials and emitted bad gases.

"They built with what they had," he said, "and they built as believers."

As for the huge, elaborate buildings they had started, he explained, the local authorities required buildings that would be impressive, in keeping with the image of a prosperous new Russia they wanted to project. Plans for lesser buildings were not approved.

"We have a great need for more new churches," he affirmed. "Billy Graham and others come and draw big crowds, but there are not enough churches to follow up with those who respond."

What about prefab metal buildings? I wanted to know. These would provide much more building for the same amount of money.

"Russians think of these as temporary, like prison chapels or church camps," he said. "They are only beginning to be accepted here."

"It is the Russian way." How many times did I hear that? We entered the partnership with Russian Baptists determined not to impose our ways of doing church on them. At times we became extremely frustrated; at other times we were forced to do some things in our own ways or lose precious opportunities.

Many times the Russian way was the only affordable way. As the city of Ryazan celebrated its 900th anniversary in 1994, the Ryazan Baptist Church was celebrating the gift of a building by the city. German Lutherans originally gave the building to the Baptists, but in 1926 the city took it from them. The University of Ryazan used it, first as a student dormitory and then to house the arts school.

When the Soviet Union collapsed, churches able to prove prior ownership of a building could apply to reclaim it or, if it no longer existed, apply for land to build a replacement. In 1993 the Ryazan Baptist Church again acquired their building, with documents verifying their ownership. However, the city required them to begin restoration work immediately and to occupy the building within 2 years—a monumental task for this poor congregation already struggling with Russia's economic chaos.

Needing more space than the building provided, the congregation decided to raise the roof 5 feet and add a balcony. Unable to obtain manufactured concrete blocks, they poured them on-site in handmade wood forms and, with the help of Kentucky volunteers, laid them around the top of the existing brick walls. To support the heightened roof they bolstered and patched the support beams with peeled logs.

Without money and materials to do a better job, the Russians do the best they can, often with amazing ingenuity. When I saw the work in progress in Ryazan, I wondered if the building would stand under its own weight. But they persevered, and in 1996 they celebrated with a glorious dedication service. A year later I saw the building again and marveled at what they had been able to do with such limited resources.

But there were other instances where the differences defied common sense. The magnificent new Vyborg Baptist Church looks striking at a distance, but a tour inside the building reveals a makeshift style of construction with materials that would not meet building codes anywhere in America.

I learned construction work from my father, who was a contractor and an expert carpenter. I shared that information with our interpreter Alexei Nikitkov; and as our construction team began work with theirs on a Monday morning in 1997, he passed that information along to the Russian builders. Before long they wanted to ask my advice.

Planning for a job seemed to take place as they started to do it. They would all gather to discuss what they were about to do, with no apparent sense of needing to get on with the work at hand. Perhaps it was the constant realization that we were with them for such short periods of time, but this frustrated many volunteers. They were into one of these "committee meetings" when Alexei called me over to talk with them. They wanted my opinion on nailing some beautiful spruce tongue-and-groove board paneling onto a wall that was the reverse side of the steeply upswept roof of the church.

Their debate was which way to turn the boards for nailing—tongue-edge up or groove-edge up. I explained that putting the tongue-edge up allowed nailing through the tongue, so that the groove of the next board would slide over it and hide the nails completely, giving a beautiful clear surface. After a long time of discussion they ignored my advice and turned the boards the other way, requiring the tedious process of driving each nail in with a nail setting tool.

After they began nailing the boards on they called me over again, this time to ask about placement of the boards. The wall was 10 feet wide and the boards were 7 feet long. Should they stagger the joints on the wall or go up the wall with a row of 10-foot boards and finish it with another row of 3-foot boards? Again that was obvious to me. Staggered joints would be much more aesthetically pleasing. But again they ignored my advice; and at the end of the day, I was exasperated when I looked in to see those beautiful boards nailed with a seam dividing them in a straight line all the way up the wall.

For 2 years after the partnership began, I studied Russian language at the University of Louisville. Though far from fluent in that difficult language, I understood enough to pick up some of what Alexei politely declined to interpret in our conversation. I understood the Russians when they smiled and discussed among themselves that I was trying to teach them "American ways." Better ways have no nationality, I thought!

Other Russian ways were cause for even greater frustration. Sometimes Russian Baptist leaders do not think in terms of outreach and future growth. They may design a building to accommodate only the present members. They may plan worship and other activities to keep traditions and satisfy tastes of present members. Such thinking will not help them reach the 60 percent of Russians who profess to be atheists and do not share their traditions.

Christian medical professionals who went to Russia envisioned treating nonbelievers as a way to show them Christian love and lead them to faith in Christ. While that happened in many cases, all too often the Russian Baptist churches planned these clinics to give priority treatment to their own members. We can forgive them, however, for what may appear to be selfishness. Under Communism, Christian believers often were denied such services. But the frustration remained for the volunteers.

To their credit, however, the Russians learned from such experiences. Perhaps the greatest benefit came to the Russian medical professionals, who gained a new way of viewing patients as they worked alongside the Kentucky volunteers. In 1996, M. A. Winchester, a family practitioner from Whitley City, and Morris Nacke, an ophthalmologist from Louisville, led a medical team to work with the First Baptist Church in Nizhni Novgorod, Russia's third largest city. Two years later I met with the medical professionals in that church.

Speaking of the Kentucky doctors, a Russian doctor said, "It was a new experience for us to talk with patients about spiritual matters. That work changed opinions of unbelievers toward Russian Baptists. Medical discussions, even with unbelievers, broadened to include spiritual concerns."

Another said, "They taught us how to treat people with spiritual help in addition to medical help—to approach healing in a holistic manner. We have been able to reach many unbelievers."

Peeled logs 60 feet long form the walls of Vizhney Volochok Baptist Church. Its wood construction and steep roof are reminiscent of an alpine lodge. Steeply pitched dormers bring light from overhead to illumine the bare wood walls and floors in the beautiful sanctuary. Kentucky volunteers recalled a half-day debate with the Russian builders over placement of the dormers, before they finally realized both were arguing for the same method.

They could not agree, however, with the legalistic approach of church leaders toward nonbelievers, and even toward believers in other churches. "There is a problem in one of our churches," the pastor remarked to a volunteer through their interpreter. "They do not require women to cover their heads in church, and some even wear makeup," he said.

Such concerns often led to judgmental pronouncements in Russian Baptist churches that divided members and alienated nonbelievers. More times than volunteers like to recall, they saw this attitude of church leaders wanting to "clean the fish before they caught them." No one denied the importance of a sincere commitment to Christ, but a judgment best left to God often was made by a church leader with much less charity.

Though this has been accepted practice throughout Russian Baptist history, Communism no doubt intensified it. KGB spies often tried to join the churches to keep tabs on who the members were and who gave significant leadership, as well as to report any activity that might be grounds for harassment or even destruction of the church. Church leaders had to be careful to prevent such infiltration. In the new Russia, however, most church leaders seemed not to have reexamined their policies.

The pastor and the deacons, usually referred to as "the brothers," lead Russian churches, often with little distinction between the roles of the two. In a typical worship service the pastor and one or two of the brothers preach, that being decided when they meet just before the service. These leaders also decide if and when someone becomes a member of the church.

Sasha is in his early 20s and very active in his church. He gives generously of his time leading children's activities, singing in the choir, and serving in numerous other roles. As we talked one day, he said something that made me realize that he was not a church member. When I asked, he assured me that he knew Christ as his Savior and that one day he would be baptized and become a member of the church. I asked when that might be. "The brothers will tell me when it is time," he said.

As one who came to Christ as a young adult, I felt sure I recognized the longing in his voice.

Such was not always the case. Things are changing in some of the Russian churches. But many Kentucky preachers delivered inspired sermons out of hearts filled with a passion to see people come to faith in Christ, only to come to the end of the worship service with no invitation offered. When people did repent—to use the Russian terminology—it was a deeply moving experience for them. Then they were supervised in a time of study and questioning to determine if their repentance was genuine. If they satisfied the brothers, they could then be baptized.

Robbie and I waited in the car while Alexei and Aram went into the train station. We had just arrived by train in Vizhney Volochok for a two-day visit in Udomlya, a city of 40,000 people less than an hour away. Udomlya was built to provide housing and other amenities for a labor force that primarily operates the nuclear power plant there. Alexei Solovyev was a 20-year-old nuclear engineering student working at the power plant when he attended the first two interpreters schools in Moscow. He also served as a kind of mission pastor for the emerging church in Udomlya. He had invited us to come and see the missions work they were doing.

Aram had driven Alexei to pick us up, and the two of them had gone to purchase our tickets for the return trip to Moscow. When they came back to the car, I offered money to reimburse them but Aram waved it away. Alexei explained that Aram wanted to do this for us—a new experience in Russia! Aram, we would learn, was an Armenian refugee from Azerbaijan. He and his family had settled in Udomlya where he had begun a shoe manufacturing business and some other profitable ventures.

When Aram's family arrived in Udomlya, his wife, Sylvia, was the only believer in the city. Though not a believer himself, Aram drove Sylvia to Vizhney Volochok to attend church there. Soon she persuaded Pastor Ghennady and the brothers to begin services in Udomlya, meeting in homes during the week and in a public square on Sundays.

A thriving congregation was developing. None of their homes could accommodate all the people at one time so groups met in different places throughout the week. Then all of them gathered for an outdoor service on Sunday. The city had given them a choice location for a new church building and recently they had begun excavation on the site.

On both nights of our visit we attended home services. During the days we visited church families and saw some of the city, including the nuclear plant. Aram drove us everywhere we went. His family hosted us for one of the evening services and for lunch on another day. We learned that he had handled all the bureaucratic details necessary for securing building permits. He had paid for the plans to be drawn and had given money for much of what they had done to that point. Aram's tracks were everywhere, yet he was not a professed believer. I questioned Alexei about this.

"He does much good, but there are some things in his life that are not acceptable," Alexei replied without going into detail. "We pray for him that one day he will truly repent."

They gladly accepted his generosity but were unable to accept him and allow God to take care of whatever personal problems he may have had. And as I saw so often in such circumstances, Aram seemed unfazed by such an attitude. Indeed, like those who made the judgment, he appeared to accept it as the way things should be.

From the first time I heard it, Vyborg didn't sound Russian. In fact, this city on the Gulf of Finland has a Swedish name, reflecting a time before Russia seized this area northwest of St. Petersburg from its Scandinavian neighbor. Perhaps because of Russia's weaker law enforcement and more relaxed morality, Vyborg's casinos and other nightlife attractions draw many tourists from Finland, only 20 miles away.

Many children in Vyborg communicate their Scandinavian heritage in their features—tall and blond, with healthy complexions. Russian children everywhere quickly won the hearts of Kentucky volunteers, but none more than those in Vyborg. Our project there consisted of construction on the new church building and Vacation Bible School—a new concept for this church.

Our busload of volunteers arrived Saturday afternoon and found that the church had other guests. A group of Swedish Baptists, we learned, had an ongoing relationship with the church and had also chosen this time for their visit. We arrived just in time to help unload used furniture and numerous boxes of food and clothes from their huge tour bus.

In the shadow of the new church building the congregation rented part of an old building for office and other use. Between the two was a school with an auditorium on the third floor. We met there on Sunday morning for a wonderful international worship service. "How Great Thou Art"—a Swedish hymn—never sounded so beautiful as it did sung by Russians, Swedes, and Americans, each singing in their own language. I preached in English, with interpreters for Russian and Swedish in different parts of the room.

But something important was missing. None of the children who were playing in the area on Saturday, and who attended Bible study earlier that morning, were in the worship service. Because this was their school, I had hoped that we would see a large number of children in worship. Instead, through the windows I could see them playing outside. When I asked the reason, I was told that children preferred to play outside. They would be bored and restless inside and, besides, church was not for that age. We had our first major challenge for Vacation Bible School.

The Swedish group had finished their work on Sunday, and half of them left on Monday. The bus engine would not start, and I will long remember the sight of 25 Russians, Swedes, and Kentuckians pushing that monster bus to jump-start it. The remaining Swedes stayed for some vacation time and we only saw them at mealtimes. We could now get started with the work we had come to do; and from what I had seen, the children were the first priority.

Word of mouth was the only promotion the church had given to Vacation Bible School, so our attendance on Monday was less than we had hoped for. But we worked hard to make it a good experience for the children, and each day attendance grew. Our team was capable and enthusiastic, and the children responded to their efforts and their love. As we approached the end of the week, bonds had formed that would make leaving a most difficult experience.

Russians love music, and the children quickly picked up the songs the team and our interpreters taught them. I asked Pastor Slava for permission to have the children sing in the service the following Sunday, and he agreed. There were over 30 of them in the service, and they sang beautifully, to the delight of their parents and the other adults.

We were excited to have them in the service, but Pastor Slava surprised us after they finished singing, announcing that the children could now go outside and play, unless they chose to stay in the worship service. Our entire team gave thanks to God when not a one of the children left. Unfortunately, we had little hope that the church would soon make any major changes in trying to reach the children for Christ.

As Russian Baptists take advantage of their freedom in the new Russia, they desperately need to learn how to reach out to unbelieving and unchurched people and to assimilate new believers more quickly into the life of the church. God is drawing them to faith and to the church like no time in recent history.

No doubt the Communist restrictions of years past have moved these long-oppressed Baptists to form counterproductive habits that will be difficult to change. Some of the differences we dealt with, such as building styles and worship styles, are primarily cultural preferences and present no major problems in their development as effective churches. But the people issues, especially those regarding the children, are a much more serious concern. Ever-increasing temptations and distractions are threatening Russia as they are the rest of the world. Russian Baptists must give their children all the help they can to resist these pressures.

Vizhney Volochok Baptist Church, 1998

Alexei Nikitkov, Misha Sokolov, and a member of Kolpino Baptist Church survey apartment buildings across the street from the church building then under construction

First Baptist Church, Nizhni Novgorod

8

LORD OF THE HARVEST

David Barnett would not return to Russia. God had used him and his wife, Brenda, very effectively there in previous missions projects, and he planned to make two trips there in 1997. Most of all David wanted to return to Vyborg because he had unfinished business in that city.

In the summer of 1996, David led a partnership team from First Baptist Church in Danville to do construction work on the Vyborg Baptist Church. Children from the area frequently came by the church, sometimes playing basketball and volleyball on the sandlot court of the school nearby, and sometimes visiting with the foreigners from Kentucky.

Yuri and Vlad were 11 and 13 years old that summer. They enjoyed watching the volunteers labor alongside the Russian workers as the beautiful new church took shape near the school they attended. As with so many Russian children, these boys seemed to have freedom to roam as they pleased, with a maturity that seemed to come with their independence.

David and the boys became good friends in the brief time of the partnership project. Much as he enjoyed the construction work at which he was so skilled, David enjoyed even more sharing his faith in Christ and made an opportunity to witness to Yuri and Vlad. Perhaps it was the Russian Baptist church's lack of encouragement for children in these decisions; perhaps it was discouragement from Russian Orthodox families; but Yuri and Vlad did not profess their faith in Christ. When David and Brenda returned to Kentucky, he vowed to go back to Vyborg the next year and follow up with the two boys.

But that was not to be. Late that year David began to have severe headaches and other unusual symptoms. Just after Christmas, Ted Garrison, a friend and team member on the project that summer, called to tell me that David was in the hospital. Shortly after that he underwent surgery, but doctors were unable to remove all of the tumor that had attacked his brain. The prognosis was not good.

Still David would not give up. He prayed that he might be able to make one more trip to Russia and continue his witness with Yuri and Vlad. When his condition grew even worse and he realized this trip would not be possible, he asked Brenda to see that someone else followed up with his two friends. And he continued to pray for their salvation.

As David fought his courageous battle, other events developed that resulted in an answer to his prayer. I had been scheduled to lead a construction team to Sosnovi Bor in mid-June, but as the time drew near, we realized it would not be possible. The project required more people skilled and capable in heavy construction work than we had. We were reassigned to a project combining light construction and Vacation Bible School—in Vyborg. As soon as I learned of my new assignment I called to assure David that I would make every effort to find Yuri and Vlad.

As we left the graveside following David's funeral that June 6, Brenda gave me a picture of David with Yuri and Vlad, taken the summer before. Ted Garrison told me everything he could remember about the boys that might help me to find them. Four days after the funeral, my team left for Vyborg.

"Oh yes," Kostya assured me, "I know both of them. Their school is not over yet and they are still taking exams. But I think they will be here next week. They sometimes attend Bible study."

Kostya worked with the youth at Vyborg Baptist Church. I had shown him the picture on the day we arrived in order to have the best opportunity of locating the boys. He did not know where they lived but felt that some of the other youth might know how we could find them.

That would not be necessary. With the children not attending the worship service, I did not see them on Sunday. But on the first day of Vacation Bible School I saw two boys who looked a lot like those in the picture. Kostya confirmed it and introduced me to them. In their early teens, both boys had grown considerably. I showed them the picture and, with Kostya's interpretation, told them of David's death and of his love and concern for them and their relationship to Christ.

Of all the experiences during my seven visits to Russia, none was more satisfying than to hear Yuri and Vlad say that they had already trusted Christ. Although they attended church, this church with its stilted traditions was not willing to do anything to acknowledge their decisions. I felt that my hands were tied at that point. Soon we would be gone and the church would be their best link to a meaningful walk of faith in the future. I encouraged them to follow through with baptism as soon as the church would permit it.

Later in the week the boys brought me a letter they had written in Russian. To be sure of an accurate translation, I asked one of the interpreters to help me write it in English. Addressed to Brenda Barnett, it expressed their love and sympathy in David's passing and assured her that they had trusted Christ as their Savior, as David had wanted them to do.

God's work in this Russian harvest was a continuing source of amazement for everyone involved. The enormity of our calling to Russia and the work we needed to do kept us constantly mindful of the need for prayer. Thousands of Baptists and others in Kentucky daily lifted this partnership to God, and thousands more in Russia joined us in a concert of prayer.

Moscow's Central Baptist Church reserves a section of the balcony for foreign guests, a tradition that began during the Communist years as a way of segregating visitors so that Russian believers could be prevented from speaking with them. That section is now an honored place where visitors always have a seat, even when many Russians line the aisles and stand for the 2-hour worship service. The first time I attended a worship service there I watched as scraps of paper floated down from the Russian sections of the balcony. People below on the main floor passed them, along with other scraps of paper coming from elsewhere in the sanctuary, to the front, where the brothers collected them and gave them to one of the ministers who sorted them into categories. Later they were lifted high as prayers were offered for all the requests the papers represented.

In services all over Russia, every time the faithful gather for worship, they repeat this custom. Russian Baptists believe in the power of prayer; and because of their influence, many partnership volunteers returned to Kentucky challenged to a more mature prayer life.

It looked no different from the other modestly painted wooden houses in this older part of the 900-year-old city of Ryazan, a 4-hour train ride southeast of Moscow. The weathered clapboards had begun to shed the blue paint from the outside. The board fence surrounding the house, once necessary to protect those who entered from prying eyes, now offered a small measure of security for the meager furnishings inside this Baptist "house of prayer."

It was a Sunday, May 1994, and a half hour before time for worship to begin people had already filled the main room and overflowed into adjoining rooms. The congregation eagerly awaited the first team of Kentucky construction volunteers who would arrive there the next month. They had already begun renovation of the church building recently returned to them by the city, but the partnership team would be a much-needed shot in the arm for that work.

Natasha Klimentovskaya, our host and interpreter, led Robbie and me to a raised platform with seats reserved for us near the pulpit. By the time the service began, people were standing around the walls and in all the rooms I could see. The atmosphere was a mixture of joyous worship and prayerful expectancy. The pastor and I preached, and other guests who had just arrived from Germany spoke. A woman led the choir in beautiful worship music using hand-copied music sheets. At the end of the 2-hour service, the pastor invited people to come to the front if they had any needs they wanted to share.

Several people responded, including a young mother holding a tiny baby. As she spoke to the pastor, she looked in my direction. I could see tears in her eyes. Natasha explained that the woman's baby was very sick and she wanted me to "bless her baby." Many times as a pastor I have been asked to pray for children who were ill, but never before had it been expressed this way. As I made my way to where she stood, I felt very inadequate for such a request. Placing my hand on the baby's arm, I could feel the heat of a high fever through the blanket wrapped around it. With Natasha interpreting, I prayed aloud for God to heal the baby and comfort the mother. And silently I prayed that God would somehow make me worthy of such a request.

It was a humbling moment—one that I and hundreds of others would experience throughout this partnership as we found God using us in ways we had not expected, to do things of which we alone were totally incapable. This labor of love called for our best and much more as we ministered. God chose to bless these people in Russia, and He had entrusted us with His power to bless.

After the service, Robbie and I were invited to lunch with the brothers and the German guests. Some of the women had prepared a hot meal and served us in one of the rooms behind the worship area. Later I went outside to find the outdoor privy that was the only bathroom facility for this house of prayer. On the way I passed by an old, unpainted shed beside the path, the door open to let in the warmth of the May sunshine. A naked lightbulb hung from a rafter giving dim light to the scene inside. An old, gray-haired man sat in a straight chair while a woman gave him a haircut using a manual barber clipper. God was also using these women of the church to bless others using their own special talents.

Volunteers went to Russia with many and varied skills and abilities. God used all those gifts as well as others He revealed in their lives in response to unexpected needs that arose while they were there. As we offered our availability to the Lord of the harvest and trusted Him, He equipped us for His work.

Kay Trisler had just dropped a bombshell on me. In one week, four women were scheduled to leave for Moscow and Nizhni Novgorod to lead a women's conference. Kay, then executive director for Kentucky Woman's Missionary Union® (WMU®), was to be the leader. She had prepared extensively and was to have much of the teaching responsibility. Now she would not be able to go. The team already had a heavy agenda, and cutting back to 3 people would create an enormous burden for them.

Kay had a replacement in mind—Delores Spears, our Russia partnership prayer coordinator. Delores already had a passport and agreed to take Kay's place, but getting a visa from the Russian government was becoming increasingly tedious, and getting one in a week would require nothing short of a miracle.

I knew better than to presume on God, but I would not fail for not trying. I called Joy Lindsey in Moscow and explained the situation. She immediately started to work there, requesting the letter of invitation from the Russian Baptist Union, hand-carrying it to the Russian officials, and sending it to the Russian embassy in Washington, D. C., by telex. In the meantime, I notified our travel agent and, through him, the visa services company that would handle things in Washington.

Delores continued to do her original partnership job in the meantime. Alerting regional prayer coordinators and others throughout the state, she explained the situation to them. For the first and only time during the entire 5-year partnership, the visa came through in one week, although it was so close that it had to be delivered to Delores en route. Our efforts proved to be even more crucial when Jenny Burris, another team member, suddenly became ill and had to cancel just before departure.

Getting Delores to Russia was a miracle, but getting her out of Russia was an even greater one! After a successful conference in Moscow, the team went on to Nizhni Novgorod for another one. The day before the team was to return to Moscow, Delores's purse, including all of her documents, was stolen. She would not be allowed to leave Russia without her passport and visa. Again we alerted prayer partners in Kentucky, who joined new prayer partners in the Russian women's conference Delores was leading. The answer to those prayers this time was even more incredible.

Joy Lindsey accompanied Delores to the police station in Nizhni Novgorod on the morning of their return to

Moscow. They had to report the theft locally and get the papers necessary to apply for a new passport back in Moscow. The team would leave the next day for Kentucky, but no one really expected Delores to return with them.

They should have! That morning, in a city of 1.5 million people, a man had seen another man throw some papers from a car window. He gathered them up and took them to the police station. When Joy and Delores reported the theft, the officer remembered the papers that had been turned in and went to get them. Among these were Delores's passport and visa! Not only did she return home with her team, but the women's conference and Kentucky Baptists also got a magnificent testimony to the power of prayer.

"You pray and you walk." Joy Lindsey gave the simple answer in response to a volunteer's question, and she was not being flippant. As they gathered in the lobby of the Izmailova Hotel, some of the team members were curious about the "prayerwalk" Joy had scheduled for the afternoon of their arrival in Moscow.

The long flight would have been tiring even without subtracting 8 hours from their day. Waiting in lines through Russian customs, a long bus ride across Moscow, and check-in and unpacking at the hotel all added to the fatigue the volunteers felt. Some of them wanted to know more about this activity that would lengthen their day even more. But this was something they needed to experience to have their questions answered.

From the hotel, the weary travelers walked just a block to the Izmailovsky Park Metro station. Jostling through the crowd down the long stairway, they passed a huge bronze statue honoring the men, women, and children who fought gallantly against the German invasion of World War II. As the train roared into the station, Larry and Joy cautioned the team to stay together and instructed them on emergency procedures should one of them get off at the wrong stop.

A half hour later they had exited the Metro at Arbatskaya station, walked through the connecting underground passageways, and emerged in the heart of Moscow. Just a short walk above ground and they were on Krasnaya Ploshchad—Red Square. The day before they had been in Kentucky, and now they stood in the center of the capital of what was known until just a few years before as the Evil Empire. It was an awesome sight!

The afternoon sun illuminated the brightly colored domes of the Cathedral of St. Basil, built in the fifteenth century by Ivan the Terrible. The onion-shaped spires cast long shadows across the red and black marble facade of Lenin's Tomb and the crenellated red stonework of the Kremlin Wall. The Savior Tower, standing astride the Kremlin Wall, held high its enormous clock in a hole so large that a Metro train could pass through it. At the end of the square opposite the cathedral stood the soon-to-be-opened Museum of Russian History, the two structures framing the open concourse like bookends. And across from the Kremlin stood the blocklong expanse of GUM, Moscow's 100-year-old shopping mall.

In the midst of this alien spectacle—in many aspects a monument to atheism—Kentucky Baptists stood and sang praises to God. The cobblestones on which they stood had borne the weight of Russian tanks and missile-carriers and felt the tramp of booted Russian soldiers marching in impressive military parades throughout the cold war. Now soldiers of Christ from Kentucky handed out Russian-language tracts telling those who came by of the salvation of Jesus Christ. The Savior for Whom the giant tower was named loved them still and had a marvelous plan for their lives.

Two policemen who may well have marched in those military parades across Red Square in years past now watched from a car parked near GUM. Now they patrolled this huge concourse, tending to an occasional drunk and keeping people away from the restricted area behind Lenin's Tomb. After a while they got out of the car and walked over to where the volunteers were singing. Instead of chasing them away, they asked if they too might have some of the tracts the volunteers were passing out. A new day in a new Russia!

Joy Lindsey had developed an excellent program for a daylong prayerwalk that she used with the participants in the women's conference earlier in Moscow. It was so well received that she had modified it to use for orienting volunteers as they arrived in Russia. As she pointed out various landmarks in the area, she used them as cues to lead the group in praying for specific needs in Russia—the Russian Orthodox Church; the government; the economy; and, most of all, the people of Russia. It was a new way of looking at this country and of preparing for the work God would use these volunteers to do over the next two weeks.

As we rode the Metro back to the hotel, I reflected on our prayerwalk experience. I had been to Red Square several times before. Had I not wanted to stay with the team, I probably would have opted to wait at the hotel and rest. But I was far more refreshed by our prayerwalk than I would have been otherwise. "It's a fantastic remedy for jet lag," I remarked to Joy.

Two months later I got a disturbing email message from Joy—the beginning of a saga that would challenge all the prayer resources of our Kentucky-Russia partnership. "Please pray for Larry," it read. "He is having some kind of allergy attack and can hardly breathe. His heart is racing and it hurts him to move. I am really concerned about him."

She had reason to be concerned. Two days later Larry was admitted to the hospital, suffering from a collapsed lung. The American Medical Clinic in Moscow offers excellent care, but something this serious is beyond their capabilities. Larry had been taken to a Russian hospital with a level of care far below that in America, and the restrictions were the same as for any Russian citizen. Because Larry was in the intensive care unit, Joy was forbidden from seeing him, talking with him, or even staying at the hospital. No one there spoke any English. Joy's only news came when she was able to speak with the American Medical Clinic doctor after he had seen Larry. Their stress level was almost equal to the seriousness of Larry's medical condition.

Joy insisted on seeing to the needs of the volunteers even while Larry was hospitalized. She said it provided therapy during the times she was unable even to hear from him. People all over Kentucky joined in prayer for both of them. Other missionaries in Russia shared the need for prayer with people in other states. By then the Lindseys were well known among Russian Baptists. Many learned of Larry's illness and shared the family's need for prayer in their churches.

The next weeks were a roller coaster of stress for Larry and Joy. His lung would heal and he would go home from the hospital. Then it would collapse again and he would be readmitted, facing the same apathetic care by medical personnel who spoke no English and the same restrictions for Joy. Eventually doctors determined that Larry needed to return to Kentucky to have surgery, but flying in his condition would be extremely risky. He would have to be medically evacuated. As visas for the foreign doctor and nurse who would accompany him became mired in the Russian bureaucracy, the Russian doctors delivered an ultimatum. Either he would be released from the hospital without his lung tube—without which he could not fly—or they would do surgery in the Russian hospital. Neither option held any appeal for Larry and Joy.

People continued to pray for their deliverance from this dilemma, and God granted their request. Just in the nick of time—on "ultimatum day"—everything came together, allowing Larry and Joy to return to Kentucky. Larry underwent successful surgery in Paducah, near their home, with his family nearby. Following a few months of recuperation, the Lindseys returned to Russia, just in time for the final year of partnership coordination.

Every project we undertook, every decision we made, every unforeseen difficulty we encountered called us to prayer. The Kentucky-Russia partnership kept us constantly mindful that this was not our work but God's. The challenge was too great for us to attempt to meet it without constant, persistent prayer. And in our praying, we grew as we saw results that could only be answers to those prayers. This was God's harvest, and we were blessed to be His laborers.

The prayers of Russians and Kentuckians loosed the power of God to do incredible things, and God worked countless miracles through the channel of prayer. As each team returned to Kentucky, the stories they shared added new recruits to an army of prayer volunteers who supported the work.

Baptism in Vyborg

Vyborg Baptist Church

Cathedral of St. Basil, Red Square, Moscow

9

HEALING AND HOPE

The liquid glowed a fiery orange as I peered into the furnace. At 1,000°F, the molten crystal flowed smoothly as the metal fingers stirred it to the proper mix. A woman pushed a long rod into the liquid and teased a mass onto the tip, lifting it out and curling the tip onto itself in one deft motion. Quickly she passed the rod with its hot orange blob to a man seated in a straight-armed chair. With one hand he rolled the rod back and forth on the chair arms, while using a pair of tongs in the other hand to force the mass into a vaselike shape. Then he passed the rod to another man who quickly twirled the still-glowing shape into a mold attached to the floor, blowing through the hollow rod as he did to create a hollow vase with a dome on top. The woman held the piece while the first man clipped it off the rod and smoothed the bottom before placing it into a box with other identical pieces. From there it would move through an assembly line for trimming, etching, polishing, and anything else necessary to create the finished piece of Dyatkovo lead crystal for which this region of Russia is noted.

Vladimir is a deacon in the Dyatkovo Baptist Church. He is also a skilled builder and serves as construction superintendent for the new church the congregation is building. By profession he is a crystal design artist, and he had invited our group to tour the factory where he works. Step-by-step he took us through the process from molten sand to finished pieces in a factory showroom. He is justifiably proud of his work. His designs are beautiful and much in demand. But he is deeply troubled by problems related to his work, problems that form a microcosm of the world as Russians know it.

The 1986 nuclear power plant disaster at Chernobyl, in what is now Ukraine, made the whole world painfully aware of deplorable conditions in one frightening facet of the chaotic economy that is the legacy of Soviet Communism. Few people realize that similar conditions, though usually on a smaller scale, plague workers in many other areas of Russia's struggling economy.

Glass particles and dust from cutting and sanding the crystal fouled the air of this dimly lit factory. Acid from etching and polishing attacked our nostrils and penetrated our lungs with heavy fumes. The high lead content, hidden so deceptively in the beautifully crafted glassware, takes its toll in employee illness and, for many, eventual death.

When I asked why people work in such conditions, the answer was both poignant and praiseworthy. To most Russians, any job, even under these conditions, is better than no job. Russians need and want the sense of self-esteem that their culture associates with a career. Occupation equals identity, in their view. For that reason most Russians stay in the same job throughout all their working years. Tragically, this loyalty often fails to bring the reward it deserves, especially as businesses and industries struggle to make the transition from government ownership to free-market operation. The crystal factory does not make a profit, so it cannot pay its employees their salaries. Instead, as payment for their labor they receive production goods which they sell on the streets at incredibly cheap prices. Then, feeling cheated by their employer, many of the employees take advantage of the factory. Customers on the street cannot tell the difference in a piece of crystal given as payment and one stolen from the factory. Consequently, 60 percent of the factory's production is lost to employee theft.

As a result, neither the factory nor the employees earn any real income. The government gets no tax revenue from either, and thus has no money to operate or to provide services to which the people are entitled. The end result is a system corrupt from top to bottom that feeds on itself and breeds dishonesty. People struggle to maintain a sense of self-worth and dignity, but find themselves frustrated at every turn.

That should be enough to discourage anyone from considering a partnership in a country like Russia. However, Jesus said of His ministry, "'Those who are well have no need of a physician, but those who are sick'" (Matt. 9:12 NRSV). Kentucky Baptists knew we would not be able to help all of these hurting people, but we could offer God's healing and hope to all those whom He allowed us to reach. Like the man and woman around the corner from Bob and Nancy Walden's apartment who stood outside in subfreezing weather to sell eggs, many people in Russia simply need a kind word to let them know someone sincerely cares for them. As this couple did, they will respond warmly to something as simple as an invitation to share a meal. And callous as they may appear at first, they are moved by the faith of people who extend such love with nothing expected in return.

Other needs are more complicated to deal with—health care, for example. Things were bad enough before the demise of the Soviet Union, but since then Russia has become a desperately unhealthy nation. Bad weather, poor diet, pollution, increased smoking, rampant alcohol abuse, and other factors combine to produce declining health and a rising death rate. Each year 700,000 more Russians die than are born. Life expectancy among Russians is 10 years less than for Americans.

Dozens of dedicated medical professionals went to Russia over the 5 years of the Kentucky-Russia partnership, and they made an impact far beyond their numbers. Doctors, dentists, ophthalmologists, medical assistants, nurses, and a host of other volunteers contributed generously of their time and other resources to show the love of Christ through their healing skills.

Lawanna Jones isn't easily rendered speechless, but Herb Booth succeeded on the Wednesday morning of their departure for Russia. "I'm in the hospital with diverticulitis," he told her. "I won't be able to go. You will have to be the medical coordinator for the team."

Lawanna couldn't believe her ears, yet she knew Herb Booth would not joke about something like that. A competent nurse, Lawanna's assignment had always been to assist the doctor. How could they have a medical team without a physician?

Herb, an active laymen from Burlington and a veteran of previous Kentucky Baptist partnerships, was a member of an advisory team which went to Moscow in August 1993. Their assignment was to assess needs and look for ways Kentucky volunteers could minister to unchurched people in the new partnership. Immediately he saw an urgent need for a wide array of medical ministries and suggested several possibilities for future projects. He volunteered his services, and a medical team with him in charge was formed to go to Tambov in August 1994. Randy Jones, then director of missions for Northern Kentucky Association, would be the team pastor, and his wife, Lawanna, would go as one of the nurses. A dentist and his assistant and two other nurses rounded out the team. With the departure scheduled for that day, there was no way to postpone the trip. Randy would take over as team leader, and they would go and do what they could without a physician.

There was one possibility of a replacement. Orson Arvin from Mt. Vernon, another partnership veteran, had returned from a project in Moscow just two weeks before. But could his visa be extended? And could he get a flight to Russia in time to arrive before the project was over? And would he be willing to leave his practice again on such short notice and go back to Russia after so recently being away?

The team arrived in Moscow on Thursday and made the 250-mile trip to Tambov by bus on Friday. They spent the weekend sight-seeing, passing out tracts, and worshiping in the Tambov Baptist Church. They knew of the effort to get Orson Arvin to Tambov for their project and they prayed that it would be successful, but realistically they knew it would take a miracle.

Monday morning the team went to the hospital where the pastor had made arrangements for their medical clinic. Randy arranged a meeting with the hospital administrator and the chief physician under whose supervision they would work. He explained the circumstances regarding a doctor—a concern for the team as well as for the Russians—and told them that every effort was being made to get one there.

The team spent the rest of the morning setting up the clinic. They took a lunch break, after which they were scheduled to begin seeing patients. As they finished their lunch, 15 minutes before they were to see the first patients, Orson walked in carrying his luggage. He put on his lab coat, held a brief meeting with the team members, and went immediately to work. Once again God had granted a miracle.

We needed another miracle. The medical team to Kimri arrived as usual at Sheremetyevo Airport in Moscow in June 1995. At the same time, a large construction team arrived at Kimri. Traveling together, the two teams had brought a dozen large cases of much-needed medicines for use with the clinic scheduled for the Kimri hospital. Customs officials, however, refused to allow the medicines into the country. The volunteers prayed for a miracle, but this time God's answer was different than what they had in mind.

After a weekend in Moscow, the two teams left for Kimri, still without the precious medicine. The medical team set up the clinic and prepared to see patients, expecting to be unable to treat many of them. They had only a few medicines from their personal luggage and a few others provided by the Russian hospital. Lisa Tapp from Finchville, one of the team nurses, was amazed as the patients began to arrive.

"Whatever we needed to treat them seemed to be there," she said. "When we ran out of one medicine, the next patients needed something else that we had."

Word quickly spread through the hospital about the presence of American doctors, and many who were already patients in the hospital left their rooms to come and be treated at the clinic. The supplies continued to fit the needs, dwindling only toward the end of the week.

Another hospital in Kimri invited the team to come for a tour of their facilities and, with some free time, they accepted. Though they were eager to learn as much as they could about Russian health care, that was not the purpose for the invitation. The doctors who gathered to meet the team had another request.

"We want to know about your faith in God," one of them said. "Will you tell us, please?"

"This is why we are here," Lisa heard one of the team members say as they left the second hospital. "The medical work is important, but telling these people about Jesus is the most important reason for our coming."

Throughout the remainder of their time in Kimri, members of the team were invited to visit in the area and tell others about their faith. Some of those they visited had illnesses that the team could not treat, but they offered comfort and they shared a witness to the Great Physician Who could minister to their deepest needs. Had the medicines been released through customs, the team might have been too busy doing good to do the best!

Kentucky Baptist medical teams always reported excellent results from their time spent in Russia. Reporting on a medical project he led to Bryansk in September 1997, Herb Booth recalled that even before the medical work began, they gave $4,000 to their host church for construction needs. Through their clinic, they saw over 600 patients and filled over 1,200 prescriptions. Despite the disappointing preference the host church gave to believers from all the area churches, the team managed to witness to a significant number of unbelievers, leading 9 of them to faith in Christ. The medical teams never lost sight of the real reason they were there. Seeing people come to faith in Christ and the joy this brings kept them going back year after year.

Herb recalled one young mother, not a Christian, who brought her 4-year-old daughter to the medical clinic, complaining that her daughter was clinging to her. The little girl's behavior was understandable when Herb heard her story. Two months before, an accident involving the little girl and her father had electrocuted the father. The child still bore fresh, red scars on her hands and back. As team members counseled with the woman about her daughter's needs and about her own grief and loss, they also talked with her about the love and forgiveness of Christ. She repented, and at the next worship service the team was delighted to see mother and daughter in the church, smiling and happy.

When the service ended, the woman told them of a wonderful feeling of freedom, peace, and joy she had experienced since she repented. She thanked them for leading her to faith in Christ. As they talked, the little girl, no longer clinging to her mother, looked up at them with her large blue eyes, smiling the smile of another one set free through the power of God.

Two people received the gift of clearer vision that morning. Jeannie Smith didn't think she would like working with the optical part of her medical team in Nizhni Novgorod in September 1996. She had always assisted the doctor and would have preferred that assignment. But she accepted her assignment of dispensing glasses and waited for her first patient to be examined. Before leaving for Russia, Morris Nacke and his assistants had read the prescriptions of hundreds of pairs of glasses donated for the project, labeling each one and packing them carefully in suitcases. At a clinic set up in the church, he examined the patients and assessed their needs. Jeannie's job was to find the pair of glasses closest to the strength the doctor prescribed.

The first patient that morning was an elderly Russian woman. Jeannie selected a pair of glasses for her and watched as she tried them on. As she looked through them, she smiled broadly; and as she looked around, she became so excited that she grabbed Jeannie and hugged and kissed her.

"Why is she so excited?" Jeannie asked the interpreter.

"She is very happy to be able to see again," the interpreter replied. "It is a miracle for her."

"And for me," Jeannie reflected later. "We take it for granted that we can buy glasses whenever we need them, but most of these people can't do that. Even if they can find them, they probably can't afford them." Then she added, "After that first day I couldn't wait for each new day so that I could fit more glasses and help more people to see."

They needed to hear as well. The Tver region north of Moscow is home to several schools for deaf people.

Industries with noise levels that would be harmful to hearing people have located there to utilize these workers who can tolerate such conditions. During 4 of the 5 years of the partnership, teams of Kentucky Baptists went to Moscow and Tver to lead evangelism projects among the hearing impaired.

Communication across the bounds of English, Russian, and two different kinds of sign language required a complex system of interpretation. Hearing-impaired Kentucky volunteers signed their messages to an English-speaking volunteer, who then spoke to a Russian interpreter. The interpreter then spoke to another Russian who knew Russian sign language and could communicate with the hearing-impaired Russians. Even with such a complicated means of communication, Kentucky Baptist volunteers still developed strong friendships with the Russians. Beth Driver, a hearing-impaired volunteer from Bowling Green, was a team member for all four of these evangelism projects. She still misses her Russian friends and prays for them daily.

"Those experiences changed my life," she said. "I believe the Lord put me there to tell them about Jesus. I am amazed at how this awesome God works out things in people's lives. I want to go back there again to keep up my spiritual life."

"Ootka, ootka, goos!" The children at Vacation Bible School in Vyborg had learned a new game, and the visitors from Kentucky had learned how to say, "Duck, duck, goose!" in Russian. While the children never tired of playing this simple game, the volunteers were usually worn out by the time they went inside for Bible study. But no one complained. The children were wonderfully responsive and attendance grew each day.

One little girl, unfortunately, was having a difficult time. Terribly shy and withdrawn, she appeared to be about 4 years old. She lived in an apartment adjoining the church office and dining hall. We assumed the woman who came out with her was her grandmother. Each day they sat outside in the warm sun on a rock near our driveway-playground. Occasionally the little girl would get up and play with pebbles or make circles in the sand. The woman, stern-faced and cold, never took her eyes off the little girl, and the girl would not make a move without looking to the woman for approval. For three days she watched longingly as the children in Vacation Bible School happily played, but either her shyness or her grandmother's reproach kept her from joining them

Josh Kansiewicz had just finished his junior year in high school in Warwick, Rhode Island. Through Kentucky's partnership with New England, he learned about our Russia partnership and volunteered to go. I invited him to join our team to Vyborg and quickly came to appreciate the natural gifts he brought to the project. His youthful enthusiasm and easy, approachable manner quickly won the hearts of the Russians. He loved working with the children, and he tried especially hard to reach out to the little girl and include her in their activities. Finally, after much coaxing, she began to respond to Josh's patient offers to play with a large ball. As she caught and returned the ball she began to laugh, but it was like a foreign, unused part of her personality. The grandmother never smiled, but she continued to watch the little girl's every move.

Obviously delighted with this newfound attention and enjoying what surely was a rare moment of play, she began to chase after Josh as the other children had done in the games. All at once, she slipped on the loose sand scattered on the paved driveway, fell down, and skinned her knee. As she stood she saw the little bit of blood that showed through the broken skin. Immediately she began to cry loudly, looking toward the grandmother who hurried to her. Showing no concern for the little girl's injury, she grabbed her by the arm and pulled her roughly to the door of her apartment nearby. Turning to say something harsh in Russian, she dragged the little girl inside and slammed the door. Then, to our horror, we heard the unmistakable sounds of beating, followed by screams from the little girl.

It was a helpless feeling for all of us. Josh was deeply shaken, feeling that he had caused this tragedy. We all assured him that it was not his fault. I felt sure that the girl would willingly have accepted even that cruel punishment for those few rare minutes of childish pleasure. The Russians were equally disturbed, but such things happened, they said, and there were no laws to prevent them and no grounds for calling any authorities. The only thing we could do at the moment was to pray, and Josh obviously needed our prayers almost as much as the little girl.

We waited a while to allow time for the woman's anger to dissipate; and while we did, we gathered up some small gifts for the woman and the little girl. As soon as we felt the circumstances would allow it, Ana Nikitkov, Robbie, and I went over and knocked on the apartment door. After a few minutes' wait the woman appeared and opened the door only slightly. With Ana interpreting, I told her that we had come to meet her and had brought some gifts.

"I do not want your gifts and I do not want to know you!" she shouted, slamming the door in our faces.

The little girl and the woman came out again the next day, sitting on the same rock in the sun. The girl had marks on her face from the beating. Occasionally she would look toward the children playing, but she never joined in any of their activities. All of us wanted desperately to try to intervene further, but the Russians said it would likely result in more punishment for the child. A happy ending for this story would be a long time away.

Fish dried in the sun, hanging close together on strings stretched across the balconies of several of the apartments. Misha parked the van in this old section of Vyborg and went around front to remove the wiper blades. He placed them inside the van "for safekeeping" before locking the doors. We walked around one of the apartment buildings and came to a door on the ground floor. A small sign identified the apartment as one of several private orphanages in the city. Vyborg Baptist Church had laid a foundation for a large orphanage next to the church, but finances now limited them to working on the church building. Until the orphanage could be built, they did what they could to help with these private family orphanages.

Smiling children greeted us and invited us inside. Though small and modest, the home was clean. These children had come to the orphanage from the streets of Vyborg. Some had been picked up by the police and brought here. Others had heard of the orphanage and found it on their own. Some of the children showed signs of abuse. No doubt others bore deeper scars. One little girl had her name scratched into the skin of her arm. The marks on her arm were healing and, from the way she enjoyed playing with the other children, we had reason to hope that whatever other marks she had were also healing.

The children asked to show us their rooms, neatly furnished with bunk beds and a few toys. The couple who looked after them seemed to make no distinction between their own children and those in their foster care. They appeared to be generous with their love. But what they could do was limited. The city government provided a small stipend for their work, but it did not go far.

We could have stayed much longer. We shared a Bible story with them, sang some songs with them, and gave them some balloon animals we had learned to make. It wasn't much, but we prayed that God would multiply it in their lives and use it to show them that we loved them.

Simple things do mean more to people who have so little. Tamara, a single psychiatrist in her mid-30s from Penza, lives with her aging parents in their small apartment. Her circumstances, more than her qualifications, dictate her meager income. At the first interpreters school she attended, I asked how she felt about that inequity.

"I have my pen and my paper and my chair to sleep in at night. I am content. After all, I have Jesus in my heart." What could I say to that?

Another time she told of an incident in the children's Sunday School class she teaches. A colleague at work had given her a chocolate bar wrapped in attractive gold foil. She took it to church to divide among the children in her class. A little girl approached her timidly.

"When the chocolate is all gone," she said, "I would like to have the wrapper to play with."

"Misha, I have a great sin in my life. Please come quickly!" The prison officer was pale and obviously frightened. Misha Petrov was their interpreter, but as a professional fireman he also was trained for medical emergencies. He followed as the officer hurried into the *banya.* There on the floor lay their friend from Kentucky. "I think he is dead," the officer moaned.

He wasn't dead, Misha quickly ascertained, just unconscious. The banya had been steaming hot, as the Russians like this combination steam bath and sauna. After a hot soak in the communal tub, the officer had administered the traditional brisk thrashing with birch branches. The Russians enjoy their banya, especially when they can share it with guests. But this had been too much of a good thing after a long and tiring week of ministry. This Russian indulgence had overcome another volunteer. He had simply passed out from the heat. Misha and the officer quickly dragged him into the shower and turned on the cold water. To the officer's profound relief, he was soon revived and back to normal.

Russians consider the banya a good way to celebrate a happy occasion, and this certainly had been a week to celebrate. The team from Clear Creek Baptist Bible College, led by professor Jim Castlen, had completed one of the most unique and effective projects of the entire Kentucky-Russia partnership. They had taken the gospel inside the prison at Borisoglebsk.

Located in the Voronezh region some 350 miles southeast of Moscow, this city has one of five prisons in the area. Beyond the other social ills that plague the country, Russia's prisons are severely overcrowded. The prison environment is dangerous and unhealthy. Trusting God for their personal safety, these volunteers shared their faith in every area of the prison, including the maximum-security area and the tuberculosis wing. Speaking to a gathering of 70 administrators and staff members, the team shared their faith and then offered Bibles to each one. As the meeting ended, the response was overwhelming as people rushed to the front to receive their Bibles. During the week, prisoners and guards alike accepted Christ. On the last day of the project, the two highest-ranking officials at the prison, Major Alexander and Captain Nikolai, also repented.

Many people are in Russian prisons for very minor offenses. Sometimes they feel forsaken and forgotten by society. While these dedicated students could not right any injustices for any of the inmates, they left Borisoglebsk knowing that many people had been set free from the burden of their sins by the power of Jesus Christ. Their return flight to Kentucky delayed, it was midnight when they finally arrived in Louisville. As I met them at the airport, I expected them to be exhausted, interested only in going home. They were all that, yet they bubbled over with the excitement of all they had experienced. When they began to open their luggage to show me the beautiful handmade souvenirs the prisoners had given them, I had to tell them it was time to go home.

Build a church and the ministries it affords may bless thousands. But healing and hope such as these teams shared happens one-on-one. In a land so vast, among people so numerous, so scattered, and often so hard to reach, it is easy to think of such ministries as an insignificant drop in the bucket. But to each person these volunteers touched, the blessing of God became real. They did as Jesus did, ministering "to the least of these."

As they look back on their places of service and their time in Russia, they can point to no magnificent structures to admire. But they know they have been instrumental in changing lives for eternity. And some of those people have reached others and will continue to do so. Only in God's good time will the results of their work be fully known. But here and now God's Word tells us that they are counted faithful for their labors.

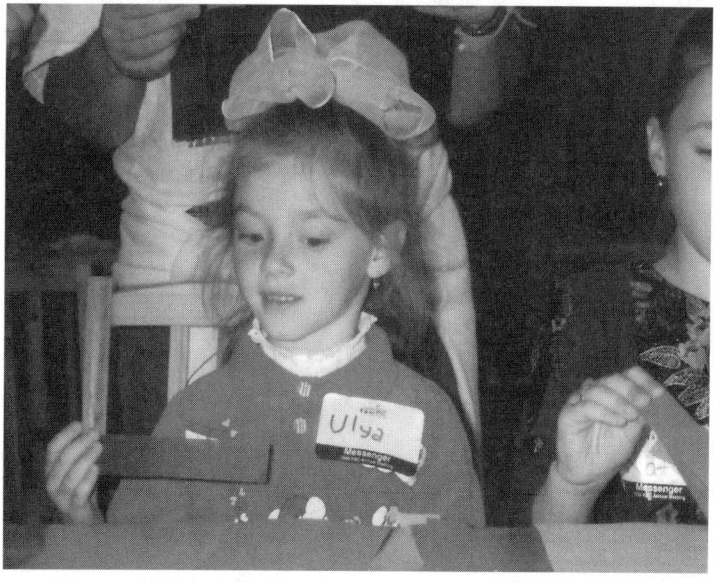

Vyborg VBS children (also next page)

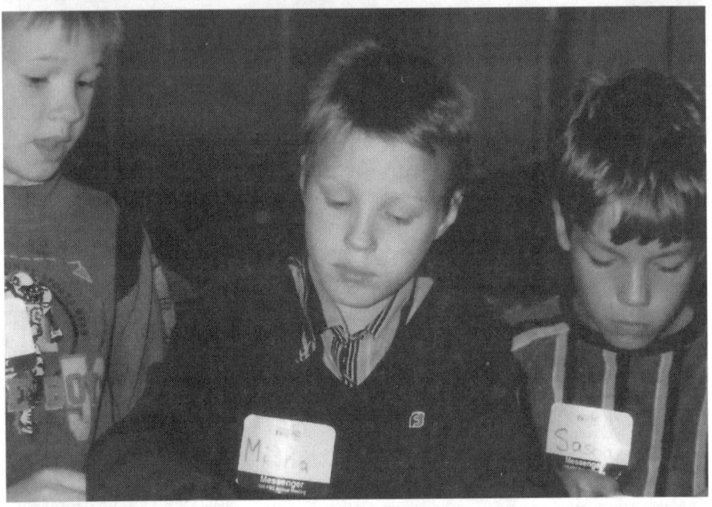

10

BUILDING FOR GOD

It was a ritual with Lonya. "It is not necessary to slam the door," he said as I closed the sliding door on the van a bit too hard. Then, reaching under the neatly folded towel in the front seat, he retrieved the cassette tape of music he had already selected. Carefully he placed it in the tape player, punched the Play button, and adjusted the volume—too loud for my taste. Then he buckled his seat belt, put the gearshift in low, and placed both hands on the steering wheel. We were ready to go.

Leonid Kotelnikov (Lonya) was entitled to his ritual. No one could have asked for a better driver or a more trusted friend. With his driving skills and his grasp of English, he was offered several higher paying jobs during the years of our partnership. Always he refused them, though, feeling called to his work with Kentucky Baptists. As he drove us northeast out of Moscow, a bizarre thought crossed my mind. Ivan the Terrible, the first Russian ruler to be crowned czar, may have traveled this same route 450 years before. Our destination, Aleksandrov, was Ivan's retreat. In 1564, when the nobles in Moscow became too loud in their criticism of his excesses, this mad Russian withdrew from the capital city, setting up his royal country residence in this charming village, where he remained for nearly 20 years.

Ivan's reign of terror is one of the darkest chapters in Russian history, and Aleksandrov was the setting for much of his barbaric rule. In what is now a fortresslike monastery, Ivan carried out mass executions and prayed for forgiveness. It was there that he staged bride shows when he was looking for a wife. And there in 1581, in a fit of rage, he killed his favorite elder son with a blow from his staff.

The purpose of our trip, however, was to see something far more impressive than Ivan's retreat. The Aleksandrov Baptist Church, called House of the Gospel, was the site of our first partnership construction project outside Moscow. First meeting in 1990, the congregation began construction on their building in 1994, and with partnership help completed the project in 1996, becoming the first Russian church Kentucky Baptists saw dedicated.

No Protestant church had existed previously in this Russian Orthodox stronghold. As we neared the church, a banner stretched across the street to greet us. Keep the Orthodox Faith, it proclaimed in bold Russian text. Before their Baptist church was organized, the handful of Baptists in Aleksandrov could only attend church in Moscow or Vladimir, 1½ hours away in opposite directions.

The building was large but not as imposing as some in larger cities. Constructed in typically Russian village style, it was sturdily built with an obvious economy of materials and furnishings. Alexei Salyonikov, pastor since the church began, was 67 and planned to retire soon. The church was doing well. Membership had reached 60, and 8 new believers would be baptized the following Sunday.

Wanting to allow sufficient travel time, we had left Moscow earlier than we needed to, arriving an hour before time for the worship service. Still, several people were already there. The crowd grew steadily; and by the time worship began that warm Sunday morning in June, the building was packed. The brothers opened windows and doors for ventilation as people filled the aisles and stood along the walls. I was invited to preach, and Valter Mitskevich interpreted for me. Afterward we celebrated the Lord's Supper. It was good to be in the house of the Lord.

A breeze stirred outside, and white petals the Russians call "summer snow" fell from trees surrounding the church, some floating inside to settle on the floor. Perhaps they were a sign of God's blessing on this special church and this special occasion.

"It was an awesome spectacle," Calvin Wilkins said, recalling the historic event. "People gathered from all over Bryansk. A brass band played rousing arrangements of hymns, some that we recognized and others with a more Russian flavor. The air was full of excitement and celebration."

It was a new beginning, a time for rejoicing. The foundation poured for what would be the new building of Central First Baptist Church in Bryansk, the congregation now gathered for worship before starting on the walls. They felt compelled to offer thanksgiving to the One on Whom they would depend if they were to finish what they were beginning. As the service reached its climax, one of the brothers picked up the first brick, holding it high over his head as Calvin and the pastor offered prayers dedicating what God would do in the years it would take to complete this building.

"It was an undertaking of incredible faith," Calvin recalled. "They had so little money. Materials were hard to find, and when they found them they often couldn't afford them. They would have to depend mainly on volunteer labor and help from their new Kentucky partners. In the past, others had promised help and never kept their promises. They hoped we would help as we said we would, but at that early date they didn't know."

Nevertheless, as the construction began on church after church, these Russian Baptists dedicated the extraordinary buildings they envisioned, believing their visions were from God and trusting Him to provide what they needed. One by one they began these church buildings—5 in the Bryansk area alone—huge imposing structures equal to the Russian Orthodox cathedrals with which they would inevitably be compared. At times these bold believers defied arbitrary restrictions imposed by governments with no sympathy for their cause, governments often strongly influenced by intolerant Russian Orthodox priests.

Members of Ascension Baptist Church in Bryansk began their building in 1987 and completed it in 1991, as the Communists were on their way out. City officials issued their permit but warned them not to build anything taller or more attractive than the surrounding buildings. Church members ignored the orders, building a beautiful church with a steeple that reached well above any of the neighboring structures. As one of the brothers told me, "We trusted God and built what was in our hearts."

They paid dearly for their defiance. From time to time police came and took away the entire congregation, hauling them off in buses and forcing them to pay stiff fines before they were released. Finally, when the builders lifted the cross to the top of the new building, the authorities stopped them. At each barrier, however, they persevered. Today the Communists are gone and the congregation worships in a beautiful building it is rapidly outgrowing.

Because of their bold faith, Baptist work is stronger in the Bryansk region than perhaps any other area of Russia. At the close of our partnership in 1998, 16 new church buildings were either completed or under construction there. Mel Skinner, the longest tenured of any of the missionaries in Russia, calls this "the one area of Russia where *Baptist* is not an ugly word."

Oryol—the word means "eagle" in Russian. As our bus rolled into this city 250 miles south of Moscow, I saw for the first time the beautiful white brick structure that is Transfiguration Baptist Church. Tall and impressive in its contemporary architecture, it easily catches the attention of motorists and pedestrians passing by on its busy street. Gleaming white brick follows striking vertical lines 3 stories high, perfectly accented with tall windows that give it an open and welcoming appearance. As I admired the angled shapes of the roofline against the cloud-strewn summer sky, I could easily picture an eagle in flight, and I wondered if the city's namesake had inspired the design of this beautiful building.

Or maybe there was another connection. Later that day as Pastor Valeriy Yeroshkin told me some of the history of this church's construction, I thought of the words of the prophet Isaiah. "Those who wait for the Lord shall renew their strength, they shall mount up with wings like eagles, they shall run and not be weary, they shall walk and not faint" (Isa. 40:31 NRSV). Possessed of a gracious and godly spirit, this man has led the church to the realization of a grand vision for God's work in this city. But he is quick to credit God for the miracles they have seen as they waited on the Lord.

Twelve people from Central Baptist Church in Oryol first caught this vision. They believed that this city of 345,000 people needed another church, so they made a commitment and began to work toward their dream. Meeting in a rented cultural hall, they grew to 120 members in just a few short years. With their new church building and with Pastor Valeriy's gifted leadership, they would soon reach many more. But getting to that point had not been easy. They were determined that work on their church building would not keep them from the more important work God had called them to do.

Before it ever had walls of its own, this church had a vision for ministry beyond its own members. They found many needs, among them a ministry to hospital patients. They paid special attention to those in long-term care who depended on such visits for contact with the outside world. One who seemed to especially appreciate their visits was a young man who was crippled, his condition such that he could do nothing for himself. These believers brought joy into his life.

As the church building began to take shape, Pastor Valeriy went to the city administration to arrange for the installation of electric service. It would require running a long electric line to the building, and, at first, the electric utility officials refused to cooperate. However, the chief administrator overheard the conversation, and when he heard the name Baptist he interrupted.

"Give them whatever they need," he said.

Later they learned that the crippled hospital patient was the administrator's son. Their electric service was connected that day and they enjoyed special treatment whenever they had further needs.

As the builders began to excavate for the foundation, they discovered that the driveway to the building site was too marshy for vehicle traffic. They desperately needed a concrete driveway to accommodate construction vehicles, but they didn't have the $2,000 it would take to build it. Pastor Valeriy went to talk with the owner of the concrete company about the problem. The man listened patiently, and after hearing the pastor's story said, "You Baptists believe people should give 10 percent of their income to the church. Give me 10 percent of the cost and you can have your driveway."

The pastor went back to report to the church. The amount was now only $200 but they did not even have that much. They held a prayer service to leave the need with God. The following Sunday as Pastor Valeriy walked to church, a friend he had not seen in a long time stopped to give him a ride.

"How are you doing, Valeriy?" the man asked.

"I am doing well," he replied, "but my church has a big problem." He explained the situation to his friend.

"Come to my office tomorrow," the man told him.

When he arrived, the man wasted no time in getting to the reason for his invitation. "It is a good thing you are doing, Valeriy. Here is the money you need," he said, as he gave the pastor $200.

Tears came to the pastor's eyes as he came to the end of his story. "I called the church together to tell them the good news and all the people wept with joy. It was

Zhatva," he recalled, their holiday in celebration of harvest time.

Stories of God's provision became legendary during our partnership. Early one morning, Pastor Pyotr Kravchuk went to talk with Larry Lindsey in Moscow. The local authorities in Bryansk had given Transfiguration Baptist Church a site for a new building, with the condition that they begin construction within a reasonable time.

"They have told us we must pay $1,000 by the end of this week to begin the foundation," the pastor said, "and we do not have the money."

Our partnership agreement did not allow us to give budget funds to Russian churches, but Larry knew that individual donors often gave money for use in partnership work. He called Calvin Wilkins to explain the situation to him. No funds were on hand, but they agreed to pray about the need.

In the mail the following morning was a check for $1,000. In the accompanying letter the donor asked that it be used for church building needs in Russia.

On another occasion, a retired pastor's wife called our office one morning to tell us of a dream she had the previous night. "I dreamed of a church in Russia that needed windows," she said. "My husband and I have been saving to buy storm windows for our home. But after I told him my dream, we decided we could do without the storm windows. We believe God wants us to give the $2,000 we have saved to buy windows for a church in Russia."

As a result, the Baptist church in Sosnovi Bor would get windows for its new building in time for winter. But the church needed more than windows. The city of Sosnovi Bor had issued an ultimatum to the church. The congregation must put a roof on the building before winter or the building would be condemned and have to be torn down.

"Not this again," I thought as I read the email message from Lee Bivins. That was in the past; this is the new Russia. They don't do things like that now, I reasoned. But there it was—an official order. Either get a roof on the building before winter or the building would be condemned.

It helped when we learned the rest of the story. There was a reason for the order. The building with its walls five bricks thick had already gone through one winter without a roof. Another winter with rain and snow freezing inside the walls would crack them, compromising the building structure and making it unsafe. That made sense, but the end result was the same. The church had to have a roof that year.

The building was magnificent so far, large and impressive, and it was in a choice location in this city 50 miles west of St. Petersburg. A military installation was within walking distance of the church. The soldiers had been ordered to help with the construction of the Russian Orthodox church being built nearby, but they were forbidden to help the Baptists. No doubt many of these soldiers would be attracted to the finished church and would then spread their witness when duty took them elsewhere.

But the ambitious undertaking suffered from the ever-present malady of these new church buildings—too little money. And for this large building, putting on the roof would require a lot of money. Kentucky's Severns Valley Baptist Association came to their rescue.

Responding to their need, John Walker, director of missions, led this association to develop a bold vision for partnership missions in Russia. In 1996 and 1997, they sent two large teams to work in Sosnovi Bor and gave over $33,000 for construction materials. They also taught the Russian builders how to build more efficiently, including hiring a crane to lift some of the heavy materials they usually hoisted piecemeal by hand. Thanks to their help, the church met the construction deadline and saved their building.

Our construction teams were usually smaller than these, and most of them gave far less money, but their projects were just as significant for the teams and for their Russian hosts.

"Let's go dig the ditch," Russ Hibbs said to his team. A veteran of previous partnership teams, Russ Hibbs had always done medical work. That was the initial plan for the project at Ramenskoye Baptist Church, but the arrangements in Russia never came together. The church did need a construction team, however, and Russ had agreed to be the team leader. Just retired from his medical practice, he and his wife, Judy, were looking forward to this project as a transition to retirement. They agreed to stay on and lead the team, even with the change in plans for the project. To say the least, the team was overqualified, as was often the case.

Renovation on the church's building was going well. Soon it would catch the attention of thousands of travelers who used the train stop just across the dirt street. The city authorities had been generous, donating a heating system and telephone service. However, the telephone connecting point was across the block directly behind the building, and the property owner behind them refused to let them cross his lot. The only solution was to dig a trench around the block.

It was not an easy job, but Russ was determined that they would get it done. No markers located lines already buried, and as they rounded the first corner, they cut the phone line to a shop across the street. The owner refused to allow them to splice the line. He demanded that they replace it all the way, adding more digging to an already difficult job. In all, the team dug 1,476 feet of ditch 1 foot wide and 2 feet deep.

As so often happened in Russia, this unexpected task proved to be a great opportunity for the volunteers to witness to their faith. As some of the team dug, others handed out tracts and answered questions as people came to watch these crazy Americans digging a ditch.

"I would not go to America to dig a ditch," the shop owner whose line was cut said to his mafia guard.

"If you were a believer like these people, you would," the guard replied.

At first the volunteers silently asked themselves the same question some of the Russian passersby asked. "Why did you come so far to dig a ditch?"

The answer became easy for them: "So that we could tell people about Jesus."

On the last partnership trip to Moscow, our group visited Ramenskoye. The pastor had contacted Larry Lindsey to ask if any money was available to help with their construction. As Larry and Calvin Wilkins closed the books on the partnership accounts, they noticed a balance of $1,200 left in the account for volunteer expenses. Our agreement with volunteers had been that any surplus funds from that account would go to Russian churches. Calvin made the decision to give this to the Ramenskoye church.

The pastor and some of the brothers were working on the church when we arrived. After a tour of the building, we walked around the block, following the route of the ditch the construction team had dug just six weeks before. The church leaders praised the team for their hard work and told us that already new people were coming to their services.

Larry had told them we were coming, but he had not said anything about the money we were bringing. Lunch was ready as we concluded our tour—soup, fat Russian sausages, bread, and noodles. After lunch Lonya, our interpreter for this trip as well as our driver, told them we had a gift for them. Before they knew the amount, Calvin asked them what they would use the money for.

"Some of the work required skills we do not have," the pastor said. "We hired two groups to work—one we paid $1,000 and the other $200. We did not have the money, so we borrowed it from the bank. We borrowed it for one month, and today is the 30th day."

The exact amount they owed on the very day it was due!

During the 5 years of the Russia partnership, more requests came for construction projects than for all other kinds of projects combined. Each is a story equally worth telling, and they continue beyond the official end of the partnership. As Tom Christopher, an accountant from Danville said, "We have unfinished business in Tikhvin." After the partnership ended, he organized two teams to help complete the church building there. Immanuel Baptist Church in Paducah entered its own 3-year partnership with the Baptist church in Klintsy, extending through 1999.

In all, our partnership assisted some 40 churches, counting construction teams and monetary gifts for construction. These will in turn help others to build, multiplying the efforts of Kentucky Baptists. And we are hopeful that Russian Baptists will soon embrace more cost-effective buildings. In three new work areas, Joe DeLeon, missionary in St. Petersburg, has convinced Russian Baptists to use brick veneer buildings with wooden scissor trusses built on-site. As these have time to prove their worth, perhaps the severely limited Russian rubles will be able to buy more buildings than they have in the past.

Even surrounded by its makeshift wooden scaffolding, the new Byezhitsi Baptist Church was an imposing sight to everyone passing by it in this busy intersection in Bryansk. Those who had lived there long had even more reason to be impressed as this magnificent building went up. Even nonbelievers knew the church's 100-year history. The Communists had regularly harassed and imprisoned its members.

In 1977 the church acquired a building permit and began construction. The KGB (secret police) protested, so the authorities revoked the permit. The church appealed the revocation all the way to Moscow, continuing to build as they awaited an answer. Late one night, the KGB had the building bulldozed to the ground. Two days later, the church received permission from Moscow to continue the building. Church members and nonbelievers alike thought it was more than coincidence when shortly after that, one KGB official committed suicide and two others died of illness.

Now the scaffolding was down. Cars and buses slowed not just for the intersection but so that people could see this beautiful new church. Soon the vehicles were halted. Some of the same police officials whose job in years past had been to harass these believers and stop this construction now blocked traffic and protected marchers for a dedication parade. Led by brothers carrying a huge Bible and a loud brass band playing spirited hymns of their faith, the church members and others marched five abreast in a procession covering the milelong route from the old church to the new one.

As the marchers reached the church, a large crowd had gathered to watch the culmination of the parade. They were not disappointed. In a clear sunny sky, a circular rainbow suddenly appeared over the steeple of the new church. An incredible sight—an awesome sign! Eighteen people professed their faith in Christ at the first service in this new church!

Yuri Sipko, assistant to the president of the Russian Baptist Union, knows well the changes the last decade of the twentieth century brought and the role Kentucky Baptist volunteers played in helping Russian Baptists reach this milestone. Speaking to a gathering of Russian and Kentucky Baptists at the end of our partnership, he said, "Not long ago many of our people were in prison. Thank God that the Communist ideology has now been broken. But many of our people are now in spiritual prisons. Now our work is before us. Thank you, Kentucky Baptists, that you came before winter. These churches you have helped us build will proclaim that God is real—God is alive. The cross on top is a witness to them of God's love."

Viktor Labko was pleased at the opportunity to show his American visitor the interior of Kolpino Baptist Church. Much of it would be ready for use soon, and he was proud of his part in the construction. He told me of his past life—events that had left him with much shame and guilt. But he praised God for the ministry of Kolpino Baptist Church, for his salvation, and for his baptism there the year before. Now he was happy to be helping build a new church so that others would come to faith as he had.

He took me to a window and pointed to a cluster of high-rise apartment buildings. "There is where I live," he said, smiling through the glow on his face. "It is a thrill for me to look out every morning and see the church. I pray for this church and for all brothers and sisters."

Joy Lindsey, Lonya Kotelnikov, and Valter Mitskevich

Aleksandrov Baptist Church, the first one completed with partnership help

11

FRUITS OF THE HARVEST

"When we began the partnership, we knew that Russia was too big for Kentucky," Pyotr Konovalchik said, "but God is bigger than Russia!"

The president of the Russian Baptist Union was in the middle of a busy day, but he was more than willing to talk with me about the work Kentucky Baptists had done over the past 5 years.

"Russian schools use a five-point scale for grading. This partnership is a five! In the beginning we did not believe this would be possible, but we were excited to dream. Many new people have been evangelized. Russian home missionaries have received support. We have many new churches, and we have many more centers for evangelism from which new churches will grow. Believers grew in number and they grew in learning how to do evangelism.

"The Russian Orthodox Church accuses us of being a church of foreigners," he added, "but that is not true. Christ has no borders, and neither does the church. We have become one family. Our church members have felt that. Kentucky Baptists and Russian Baptists became one body together."

Indeed we did. And though the partnership has officially ended, neither Russian Baptists nor Kentucky Baptists will ever be the same again. Too many good things happened.

•Pastor Ernest Martin of Danville recalled a partnership trip in which 157 people professed faith in Christ, including one man who publicly repented during the offering in a worship service.

•Fred Miller, a bivocational pastor, challenged Friendship Baptist Church near Campbellsville to give $1,000 for a church building in Russia. They refused, voting instead to give $5,000 plus additional support for a Russian home missionary.

•A Russian newspaper reporter came to interview a Kentucky volunteer team. After hearing the gospel proclaimed, he accepted Christ. As one team member said, "He came to cover the news and left with the good news."

•During the Soviet years, young people in Russia often attended Communist youth camps. Capitalizing on that history, Christian camps now draw large numbers. Instead of the 100 expected at one camp for teenaged girls, 650 attended. Fran Morrison, wife of team leader and Little Bethel Baptist Association director of missions Bob Morrison, watched children climbing the walls on latticework to hear about Jesus. She said it reminded her of the story of Zacchaeus climbing the tree to see Him. Over 500 of the teenagers attending this camp made professions of faith in Christ.

•A construction team led by James Jones, pastor of Campbellsville Baptist Church, and including then-Kentucky Baptist Convention (KBC) president Billy Compton, arrived in Kolpino to find that the church had failed to secure the necessary building permits. Remembering the watchword of partnership missions—Flexibility—and employing the diverse talents of team members, they organized Vacation Bible Schools, distributed Bibles, and ministered in hospitals and even an abortion clinic. Several volunteers had opportunities to share their faith in workplaces corresponding to their own occupations.

•Billy Compton recalled a hospital visit in which an old woman began to cry. Concerned that he might have said something to hurt her, he and an interpreter asked why she was crying. "I have been a believer many years," the 80-year-old woman said through her tears, "but I have never had my own Bible. God used an American to bring me a Bible."

•Ghennady was already retired when he attended the interpreters school in Moscow. Encouraged and emboldened to share his faith, he went to visit his former schoolteacher, then more than 80 years old. When he told her who he was, she remembered him. "You were the boy who caused me so many problems with the authorities because you were a believer," she said. As he concluded his visit, he asked if he could pray for her. Following his prayer, she then prayed for the first time in her life, repenting and becoming a believer!

•Mikhail, a teenaged believer and interpreter from Udomlya, was eager to share his faith with his unbelieving English teacher. He took his English Bible to her with words underlined that he did not understand. "Will you explain these words to me?" he asked her.

•Inspired by the outreach methods of Kentucky Baptist volunteers, members of Byezhitsi Baptist Church developed an evangelism plan for the 170,000 people in their area of Bryansk. They call it Home to Home. They spent six months creating a detailed map showing all of the houses and apartments in their section of the city. Each month, they distribute 3,000 invitations to nonbelievers in a targeted area to attend a nontraditional, seeker-type service. Ten percent of those receiving an invitation generally respond, and of those, the church baptizes 10 to 15 new believers each month. They plan to reach all 170,000 people in 3½ years and have a goal of doubling the church's membership every 2 years. They are right on schedule, filling their beautiful, new 1,000-seat church building twice each Sunday. Thirty of the brothers recently completed training in the church's Bible study institute and are working with small groups to plant new churches in the area. The church's specialized ministries include outreach to deaf people, led by a young deaf couple. That ministry has grown to 10 people each Sunday. One Sunday a deaf woman used sign language to share a poem about Christ. A deaf man who came to church that day said, "If the deaf glorify God, He must really exist."

•Across town in Bryansk, Central First Baptist Church gathered for worship on a Sunday night in October 1998. Soon they would be ready to move into their beautiful new building, for which we had delivered to them a gift of $4,000 for the purchase and installation of a heating system. Now the harsh winter coming on would not damage the building, and the finish work inside could continue on schedule. From the pulpit area I looked out over the congregation. They still followed the tradition of many older congregations in which all the men sat on my left and all the women on my right. I hoped that would change as they moved to the new building.

•As he worked with Kentucky Baptist volunteers, Nikolai Sirovatka learned a new concept for a new day in the Russian Baptist church. He caught a vision from God for education ministry with the children in the St. Petersburg area. Children who had been excluded from church during the Communist era now could enjoy the church activities to which they were naturally attracted. Pouring his heart and life into the ministry, he is teaching the concept to every church that will listen. Even after the official close of the Kentucky-Russia partnership, donors continue to send money to help reach these children through his work. "Like Thomas who could not believe without touching Christ's wounds," he said, "some people must touch walls to give. But some in Kentucky had faith to give without seeing walls. Education ministry is only a seed in Russia, but it is growing thanks to the help of Kentucky Baptists."

So many seeds, planted, growing, and bearing good fruit.

As the van rounded the long curve in the road, I looked over Lonya's shoulder and saw the steam rising from the cooling tower of the nuclear power plant. It was good to be back in Udomlya. It had been over 4 years since Robbie and I first visited these warm and friendly people and shared their dream for a new church building. The streets still looked familiar and I knew we were nearing the church. As we drove past the police station and turned into the driveway, a lump came into my throat.

What had only been a huge hole in the ground when Robbie and I visited in 1994 was now taking shape as yet another beautiful Russian Baptist church. Several Kentucky teams had worked here, and volunteers and their churches had given generously to buy construction materials. The result was another miracle in the making. Pastor Ghennady from Vizhney Volochok was hard at work on the building, as were several others. Beaming at the opportunity to show off this work in progress, they interrupted their labor long enough to give us a tour.

The pastor then directed us to a small wooden house nearby, a red frame building that had obviously once been someone's residence. As we got out of the van, I saw the sign high up on the wall facing the street. House of Prayer, the hand lettering proclaimed, Church of Evangelical Christians—Baptist, Udomlya, Tver District—the official identification for this Russian Baptist Union congregation. They were growing. On my previous visit, small groups met in members' homes during the week, and everyone gathered outdoors on Sundays when weather permitted.

As our group got out of the van, I recognized a familiar face outside. Aram was lighting a fire of crisscrossed wood. They were expecting us for dinner, and our arrival was his cue to start the fire for *shashlik*—the delicious barbecue

Armenians love. Inside, Aram's wife, Sylvia, and their two daughters, almost grown since I last saw them, were busy preparing the rest of the meal. It was a delightful reunion.

The meal was wonderful, with an abundance of food and great fellowship with Pastor Ghennady and the brothers who joined us, along with Aram and his family. We discussed the progress on the church building and their projection for completing it. Kentucky friends had learned that the church needed money to roof the new building before winter and had sent a generous gift with us—more than they had requested. Through tears of joy they assured us that getting the roof done in time would be *nye problyema*—no problem!

But the best was yet to come. As we talked around the table after the meal, I asked about Aram's two sons who were not present, and he asked about Robbie. I was surprised to learn that they had put our picture on the wall of their home. Sylvia told our group that she had been the only believer in Udomlya when they arrived from Azerbaijan and felt great joy in knowing that soon they would have a new church in which to worship in Udomlya.

"But my greatest joy," she said with tears coming to her eyes, "is that Aram has repented." Her husband, who had done so much for us on our previous trip and had helped the church in countless ways before his repentance in the church, was now officially a member. He had dealt with whatever had been lacking in his relationship with God and the church. The smile covered his whole face as we rejoiced with him.

Alexei Solovyev arrived just as we were about to leave. Seeing this dear friend once again made the day complete. I knew him from the interpreters schools in Moscow and from my previous visit to Udomlya. He now serves as pastor of the church, along with his full-time job at the nuclear plant. He had married and had a son since we last saw him, and he gave me a picture of his family to take home to Robbie.

The long drive to Udomlya and back had taken the whole day. As we drove southward over the high bridge spanning the Moscow River, my mind drifted in peaceful weariness. The setting sun ahead of us painted the clouds with bright hues of red and orange, the colors spilling down onto the apartment buildings across the river. I looked out my window toward the setting sun. As the bright orange ball dipped below the rolling hills in the distance, a brilliant array of golden sunbeams formed a crown above the now darkening western clouds. A perfect ending to a glorious day.

"It is impossible to translate," Sasha (the interpreter) said, grinning and shaking his head. "It means very good, faithful, sacrificial! All of that." I had asked Yuri Sipko, assistant to the president of the Russian Baptist Union, to assess the partnership from his perspective as assistant to the president of the Russian Baptist Union. His praise was effusive as he reflected on the work of Kentucky Baptists in his beloved country.

"When Jesus left heaven to come to earth, people took heart. They were encouraged to follow Him and do the things He taught them. In a time of persecution and problems for Russia, people whom we did not know came from Kentucky. They took up bricks and shovels, building houses of prayer. They told unbelievers about the love of

God. It was 'faith in action.' Our people wanted to do the same things they saw Kentucky Baptists doing. We caught your fire and we wanted to go to work!"

The fire was from God. And how it burned in Russia and Kentucky!

Marty Logsdon had never shared his faith one-on-one before he arrived in Russia in May 1995. As he got off the elevator in his Moscow hotel, God provided the opportunity and the courage for his first effort. On each floor in the hotel, a "key lady" exchanged room keys for registration cards when guests went to their rooms, reversing the exchange when they left. Marty decided to talk to the key lady.

Using materials printed in Russian and English, he tried awkwardly to communicate with her, and she seemed to respond positively. To be sure she understood him and the tract she was reading, Marty went to get one of the interpreters to translate the conversation. The woman had been troubled over a family matter and had been praying for God's help. She saw this as an answer to her prayers, and she repented and professed her faith in Christ.

Further encouraged, Marty found other opportunities during the project, leading others to repent and confess their faith in Christ. Through his experiences in Russia, he began to sense God's call to vocational ministry. He later enrolled in a Bible college and became pastor of a church. He hopes one day to become a career missionary.

Marty was not the only volunteer to experience God's call to vocational ministry at least in part through their partnership missions involvement. Others drew closer to God and learned better how to live their faith. As Gayle Boyle, partnership volunteer to Bryansk in 1997 said, "I discovered a brand-new level of spirituality in my life."

The blessings Kentucky Baptists enjoyed as a result of this work were every bit as rich and as numerous as those the Russians experienced.

Four young girls from Perryville Baptist Church set up a booth at Forkland Community Festival and sold handmade items to raise money for Bibles to send to Russia. In 1996 they raised over $700 to send with Tom Christopher's team to Tikhvin.

"If you give your time and talents, we'll pay your way." Harold Greenfield made that offer to potential volunteers on behalf of Caldwell-Lyon Baptist Association. And they kept their word, sending over 30 volunteers to Russia while also supporting volunteers going to other areas. At times travel bills were due before sufficient contributions had come in from the churches, and the association borrowed money to pay them. "Sometimes we had a noteburning at the same time as our commissioning service," Harold said. But their commitment to missions involvement has led to increased giving to all causes from churches throughout the association.

In an inspiring letter to the Kentucky Baptist newspaper, *The Western Recorder*, Jamie Broome, pastor of Immanuel Baptist Church in Paducah, wrote of his experience in Russia: "I don't believe I will ever be the same again. . . . I have begun to see the world differently, recognizing that it is my Father's world which He is seeking to redeem. Seeing the world as my Father's, I am now gaining new insights into what the church is called to be. My mind is changing. I am repenting."

When Dennis Adams, a member of Broome's team to Klintsy in 1996, was asked if he saw anyone saved in Russia, he replied, "I saw 15 Americans saved."

We counted the number of volunteers—1,503 over the 5-year span of the partnership. But only God could count all the blessings Russians and Kentuckians experienced in this magnificent venture of faith.

Though some of the recollections seem less profound than others, they are memorable nonetheless. Many Kentuckians left part of their hearts in Russia. Floyd Price, then-president of the Kentucky Baptist Convention, left part of a finger, the result of an encounter with a crude electric planer in Ivanovo. Calvin Bohannon of Hardinsburg was offered a parcel of land in Dyatkovo by none other than the city's mayor, if he would agree to stay and farm it. Concerned with his bachelor status, his Russian hosts assured him that they could also find him a wife!

The blessings of this partnership spilled across the borders of Kentucky. Volunteers outside the state joined several teams, and many others gave money and supported the work with their prayers. Barbara Smith from Collierville, Tennessee, knits mittens from leftover yarn. Through the daughter of our office secretary, Carla Purvis, Barbara heard about our partnership work and donated hundreds of pairs of mittens to warm the hands of Russian children.

To the volunteers who made that long journey of faith, Russia became people. No longer was it some strange land whose mention called up vague images of frozen land and cold war. Russia became people—people who love and need love—and most of all, people for whom Christ died and to whom we must take His good news. Michelle Wright, a seminary student from Florence, plans to become a career missionary. After a trip to Udomlya in 1997, she described her impressions in a beautiful poem that she granted permission to include.

MOTHER RUSSIA

Today I saw Mother Russia.
Not marching through Moscow's Kremlin,
Not against a yellow brick background,
Not landing on a gymnast's mat,
Not pirouetting across a Bolshoi stage.
I saw Mother Russia, scarves on bowing heads, tired eyes closing. I saw working hands grasping plastic bags, worn with use, containing a day of life. I saw working hands, thick hands, right hands, ring fingers banded.
I saw feet, calloused from walking blocks. Miles. Days. Years. Lives.
I saw broad, hunched shoulders, burdened with their country's hardships and toils.
I saw swaddled babies. Many mouths to feed. Many meals to prepare. Many dachas to tend. Much work done. Much work doing. Much work to do.
Today I saw Mother Russia.

"There's been an explosion in the Metro." The voice on the phone belonged to Calvin Wilkins. His call came to my home early that morning, long before time for me to leave for the office. "Larry Lindsey called me at home at 2:00 this morning to tell me. He's talking with the other missionaries about it now. We may have to cancel the teams leaving today."

I hurried into the office, troubled by the news and wondering what would be the best course of action. It was June 12, 1996. Boris Yeltsin's reelection was the hot topic in

Russia, and I had no doubt this was a political act. But how big was it? Was this part of some widespread terrorist plot? Was it an attempt to take over the shaky Russian government? Or was it just an isolated incident? Two Kentucky Baptist volunteer teams were scheduled to leave for Moscow that morning. One thing was certain: we had to make a decision soon.

By the time I got to the office, we had additional information. The bomb had exploded on the Gray Line of the Metro, between Tulskaya and Nagatinskaya stations—the two stations nearest our Moscow office and the Russian Baptist Union. People had been killed. Our coordinators traveled that same route every day. No further incidents had been reported, but Americans were being advised to keep a low profile and avoid going out in public.

We could not risk the safety of our volunteers. We concurred with the recommendations from Moscow and called off our two projects. We would absorb the loss from nonrefundable airfares and other costs. And we would reschedule volunteers who were available for later projects.

No further incidents developed, as it turned out. But God brought great good out of that event.

One of the teams turned back that day was from Lynn Baptist Association, scheduled to do evangelism work in Aleksandrov. Lonnie Sheets, their director of missions, had been to Vizhney Volochok in 1994 and had come back excited about the partnership work. He led this association to give sacrificially to support the team that now was unable to go. But he and his association were not discouraged. If anything, the cancellation of their team's trip inspired them even more to be involved in this work in Russia. They became one of the strongest associations in the state in support of partnership missions.

Gerald Murphy, pastor of Munfordville Baptist Church, was among the volunteers on that team. He had taught in the pastors school in St. Petersburg the year before, and he was looking forward to leading a team to do evangelism work through this project. Although he was disappointed when I called to tell him of the cancellation, he understood and agreed to reschedule his trip and join another project. That opportunity came four months later. God wanted Gerald to go to Bryansk.

The project at Bryansk involved an excellent medical team, but they needed a pastor. The association approved, and Gerald agreed to go. Then another need arose. One of the nurses had to cancel at the last minute and the team needed a replacement for her. I knew that Sheila Murphy, Gerald's wife, was a nurse, so I called to ask if she could go. God wanted *both* the Murphys to experience Russia, especially Bryansk.

Gerald and Sheila both returned from their trip believing God had more in mind for their missions work than short-term projects. The next year, Gerald returned to Bryansk to lead a construction and evangelism team. When he returned, he told me in confidence that he and Sheila felt God calling them into career missions. They would not tell their church family until they knew they were approved for missionary appointment.

Gerald kept in touch with me through the application process, and we rejoiced when he and Sheila were approved as career missionaries. At their commissioning service in September 1998, Gerald spoke of his partnership missions experiences. "It was in those three life-changing investments that I have come to know God's call," he said.

In March 1999, the Murphys completed missionary orientation and moved to Moscow to begin language study.

Their next stop, their new missionary assignment? Bryansk—continuing the work that Kentucky Baptists began in Russia!

"Twenty years ago, if we had invited you to Russia, it would not have been possible for you to come," Pyotr Konovalchik said. "But now God has opened a door and you have come. You lived in our homes, you ate our food, you saw our circumstances. You gave money, and you came and built with your own hands. You taught our people and encouraged them. They said, 'We should be doing that.'

"Your work has left a strong foundation for Russian Baptist work. You have left a great chapter in the history of Russian Baptists."

Udomlya Baptist Church construction, 1998

12

MY LORD, WHAT A MORNING!

"Did you have mosquitoes in your room?" Valter Mitskevich asked hesitantly. Never one to complain, he as a child had lived hand-to-mouth while his father was imprisoned by the Communists. In his 60-odd years he had seen real suffering as a minister working amidst persecution and deprivation. But the mosquitoes *had* been terrible.

Just outside the windows of our guest rooms stood a large greenhouse where our host grew beautiful roses. It was much in need of repair, and the recent rains had left lots of sheltered pools in which these buzzing demons could reproduce. All night long they had kept Calvin Wilkins and me holed up under the covers, in between desperate attempts to reduce their numbers with flailing towels.

But the morning promised better things by far! It was Sunday—the long-awaited day for dedication of the new Seltzo Baptist Church.

For the past several days the entire congregation had worked like beavers to complete the last details on the beautiful building. As the choir rehearsed inside the night before, others were outside smoothing hot asphalt in the parking lot. As if that were not enough, the women had set up the long dining hall that same evening and served a bountiful dedication banquet to visiting guests from the surrounding areas. Calvin and I were among the guests, as were Larry and Joy Lindsey and Kentucky Baptist Convention (KBC) president Gayle Toole and his wife, JoAnn. This was the closure tour for the Kentucky-Russia partnership, and the Seltzo dedication service that Sunday morning promised to be a highlight.

The final year of the partnership was a bittersweet time. The consuming events involved in choosing two new partnerships to follow our partnership with Russia had not diminished my feelings for these people and this country that I had come to love so deeply. They were a part of me and I of them, and that would not end with the conclusion of our work together. There were some victories to celebrate and some encouraging signs as we prepared to say good-bye.

If Moscow is the face of Russia, a smile came to that face as the city celebrated its 850th birthday in September 1997. The transformation was incredible! CNN had accepted Moscow's invitation to the big event and its satellite broadcast would put Russia's ancient capital on center stage. Mayor Yuri Luzhkov declared that Moscow would lead Russia "to achieve the greatness and the power that we have the right to declare to the whole world."

The funeral for national hero Yuri Nikulin, beloved clown, actor, and circus director, had left all of Russia weeping just the week before. But even that did not slow the preparations for Moscow's celebration. By mayoral decree, every business had a birthday display commensurate with its size. Every building in the heart of the city was brought into good repair, with exteriors cleaned and freshly painted. Workers came from other countries to help local laborers meet the deadline. A new three-level underground shopping mall with upscale stores and an American-style food court opened in the shadow of the Kremlin. Billboards all over the city displayed messages of love and good wishes for the city: My Moscow; I Love You, Moscow; Happy Birthday, Moscow. Over the picture of a baby pointing, the caption read, "Maybe I'm not the mayor, but I care."

For three days, Muscovites celebrated this grand occasion with pageants and concerts in Red Square, a laser light show in the Lenin Hills, a parade down Tverskaya Street, and numerous other events. As the world watched Moscow pass this milestone, perhaps it would now see her as the modern world capital she so wanted to be.

The highlight of the celebration for believers came with the consecration of the new Cathedral of Christ the Savior. Mayor Luzhkov, who had worked tirelessly to rebuild the cathedral, spoke at the consecration. "Our strength is in unity and in our faith," he proclaimed—new language for a new Russia!

You couldn't blame them. The temperature soared and the paving stones reflected the bright sun. They were just trying to cool off the only way they knew how. Stripped to their underwear, they cavorted in and out of the water as a policeman tried halfheartedly to chase them away. They were having too much fun.

The series of pools and fountains that separated the new underground mall from the Kremlin grounds was Moscow's gift to itself. The large bronze figures from Pushkin's fairy tales invited the frolicking, and the water was cool and tempting. Finally, frustrated at his vain attempts to chase the revelers out of the water, the policeman shed his shoes and shirt and joined them.

Such serendipity is new to Moscow. A decade ago, authorities would not have dealt with such defiance so lightly. But it was a welcome sign—a new way to deal with old problems. And there were others. Russians possess an incredibly resilient nature. How else could they put aside the worries of a chaotic economy and an inept bureaucracy to relax and enjoy themselves this way?

And their troubles don't go away. A year later I sat at the table in the home of Nikolai Romanyenko, beloved superintendent of the Bryansk region. I listened as he and Valter Mitskevich discussed the economic crisis in Russia—workers not getting paid, or receiving production goods and promissory notes; rampant inflation; a mood of desperation and hopelessness. They feared that some kind of revolution might be inevitable. If someone should capture the imagination of the people, the people might follow, no matter how radical or destructive the ideology they espoused.

The answers are not political. The revolution they need is spiritual.

Our host's home was only a short distance behind Seltzo Baptist Church. As we walked up the street toward the front of the church, I could hear voices murmuring in a kind of reverent anticipation. The atmosphere was charged with excitement. As I rounded the corner of the church, I found the street already crowded with people milling about. More had gathered in the parking lot on the other side of the church.

Many admired the building, with its brick-Gothic design trimmed in ornate metalwork forged at the hands of Moldavian craftsmen. Striking vertical lines reached up to a gleaming roof of galvanized metal with a high steeple topped by a cross. Inside, paneled, horizontal wallboards of light spruce peaked in vaulted Gothic arches 30 feet above. Sections of decorated plaster accented the wood walls, with Scripture verses stenciled behind the pulpit. This church building conveyed a sense of importance and permanency that would not easily be discounted by those who wanted to discredit these Baptists.

Fifteen minutes before the start of the service, a 40-piece brass band began to play a rousing selection of lively hymns. People hurried about, tending to last-minute details. One of the brothers called us to come into the dining hall and line up for the procession. Lines had formed outside the rest rooms. The service would begin at 10:00 and was scheduled to last until 2:00.

We joined the pastors and the brothers for prayer, then moved outside for a procession into the sanctuary through the front entrance. It was an incredible sight! People had already filled the church to overflowing, crowding in windows, aisles—anywhere they could sit or stand. There was no way for us to get inside until the brothers ushered people out of the center aisle long enough for us to enter.

The brass band joined the choir inside. As they combined in a processional hymn, the pastor raised his Bible over his head and led us inside to a section of chairs reserved for us on the platform. As we reached our seats, I could see there was no room for anyone else inside the sanctuary. The sense of expectancy and celebration were overwhelming. "I don't expect to see anything like this again until Jesus returns," Calvin said as we sat down.

Choirs, ensembles, soloists, and instrumentalists provided beautiful music. In the Russian tradition, speaker after speaker preached or brought greetings—16, if I counted correctly. Pastors from area churches had left preaching responsibilities to the brothers in their churches to come and join this celebration.

Neighboring pastor Pyotr Kravchuk had waited a long time for this moment. At times the wait had been incredibly painful. He recalled how the Communist authorities had ordered him to stop preaching the gospel. When he refused, they came and took him to jail. They grabbed his necktie and dragged him into a cell, where he almost choked to death before someone found a knife and cut the tie from his neck. To this day he refuses to wear a necktie except on special occasions such as this.

Pastor Kravchuk remained in prison for 2 years. During that time people from America—he never knew who they were—sent packages of food and clothing to his family. They survived only through that anonymous generosity. "This is from America," the Russian postal official said to Pyotr's wife once when she went to pick up a package. "They are your enemy. You should refuse to accept the package."

"My enemy is the one who put my husband in jail," she replied as she took the package.

Heads nodded in understanding as men and women wiped tears from their eyes on hearing Pyotr's story. This moment had been long in coming, but it was here and that was all that mattered. Soon another magnificent church—Transfiguration Baptist Church where Pyotr Kravchuk was pastor—would be ready for dedication.

Like Gideon's army, the numbers of these Russian Baptists were small, perhaps for the same reason. They celebrated a victory in Seltzo, one that has been and will be repeated over and over. No one could doubt that it came from God. The faithful pastors who serve these Russian churches have endured persecution and hardships we can scarcely imagine. Most of them work at secular jobs in order to serve congregations that can barely pay utilities, much less a pastor's salary. They believe in a God of miracles, and they trust Him for their needs.

Nikolai Romanyenko used Scripture on this occasion to speak for all of them. "The steadfast love of the Lord never ceases, his mercies never come to an end; they are new every morning; great is your faithfulness. 'The Lord is my portion,' says my soul, 'therefore I will hope in him'" (Lam. 3:22–24 NRSV).

"Joy and tears," Yuri Sipko said as he expressed his feelings at the close of the Kentucky-Russia partnership. Indeed. In visit after visit we stood facing the congregation at the close of a service. "God be with you till we meet again," they sang in Russian, and through our tears we attempted to join them in English. They waved handkerchiefs and wiped tears I will never forget. Russia will never let go of my heart.

The people are Russia's heart, and I had attempted to say good-bye to them, albeit with little success. Now there was Moscow. Beyond question, it is very different from the rest of Russia. By Western standards underdeveloped, but still it strides at the head of Russia's slow march toward an elusive future. Moscow had become for me the face of Russia—the point at which I could connect with this land in its broader concept. I needed some time to look once again at Russia's face and try to say good-bye.

Pastor Leonid Sergienko of Khimki Baptist Church invited us to dinner, but I declined, leaving Calvin, Larry, and Joy to visit with this charming family. I boarded the Metro at Dobryninskaya station, once again burrowing deep underneath this city as I had so many times before. I had long since learned my way around the Metro system enough to be at ease traveling alone, and in the last couple of years, my understanding of Russian allowed me to recognize the stops when they were announced. That freed me to concentrate on the people.

Their faces and what they carried told many stories—or none—as I looked down the length of the clattering Metro car. Some hid behind books with dust jackets made from folded newspapers. Some dozed. Others stared blankly across the car. The ubiquitous plastic shopping bags held who knows what. Designer clothing with misspelled names and crude copies of American logos—a baseball cap touting loyalty to the New York Bears—betrayed the Russian admiration of Western goods. Neat bouquets of flowers promised an enjoyable visit with a friend. Young people leaned against each other face-to-face, talking quietly of things far removed from the troubled world above them.

Oktyabrskaya station came at the next stop. I entered the street at the Varshava Hotel, across from the huge statue of Lenin. Trolleybus number 7 took me up the long hill past the residence used by Nikita Khrushchev and past the huge statue honoring cosmonaut Yuri Gagarin. I got off at the top of the hill.

Moscow State University stands tall and imposing a block away—one of seven identical buildings Stalin had constructed. But the view in the opposite direction was what I came for. Russian author and dramatist Anton Chekhov said, "You cannot know Moscow until you have seen it from here." From this vantage point, one-sixth of Moscow spreads out in a spectacular panorama.

Looking across the bend of the Moscow River and past the Olympic stadium, I found familiar landmarks in the distance. Off to the left was the White House, seat of the Russian government. To the right of it, the huge golden dome of the Cathedral of Christ the Savior caught the afternoon sun. Just beyond it several smaller golden spires located the Kremlin complex. And off in the distant haze Ostankino Tower beamed its radio and television signals from 540 meters above the city.

For a long time I stood there drinking in the view. As these and other landmarks brought to mind different facets of the city and the country, I asked God's blessing on them one by one. After a while I caught the trolleybus to continue my journey past the Victory Memorial Complex and the Triumphal Arch. I changed to the Metro, completing the circle back to the center of the city. One last time I wanted to touch this face up close.

Exiting the Metro at Lubyanka station, I came up through Dyetski Mir, the huge toy store, and out to the street, turning toward Theater Square. As I walked down Teatralnaya Prospekt, past the Mali Theater and the Bolshoi Theater, I wondered how Russia could be so rich in things artistic and so poor in social and economic areas. The street narrowed and angled slightly left to become

Okhotny Ryad, and I walked past the Duma where the Russian legislature meets. I had tried to go in one time but a guard turned me away, informing me that there were no excursions that day.

I turned left past the hotel built for Stalin with two different facades on either side. Legend says that the architects were not sure which design Stalin favored so they built one of each to be sure of pleasing him. To my right across the plaza, light showed through the domed skylights of the new underground mall. The afternoon was becoming evening.

Crossing the marker identifying the center of Moscow, I turned and looked down Tverskaya Street. The arrow on the marker pointed northwest toward St. Petersburg. Turning back, I continued through the newly rebuilt Resurrection Gate and on to Red Square. Shoppers hurried in and out of GUM to my left. The sun had abandoned the Cathedral of St. Basil as I reached the other end of the square. I looked across the Big Moscow River Bridge, remembering the German teenager who had landed his small plane there, confounding Russian border defenses.

Turning back, I paralleled the massive Kremlin Wall, past the Savior Tower with its huge clock. As I passed Lenin's Tomb, I noticed that the ruby-colored stars in the towers were already aglow against the darkening sky. Over the wall I could see the top of the Grand Kremlin Palace where Russian leaders entertain visiting dignitaries. As I reached the massive black and gold wrought iron gates I turned left, following the Kremlin Wall into Alexandrovskiy Garden.

The light breeze danced with the eternal flame burning in the Monument to the Unknown Soldier. Small bouquets of flowers lay around its perimeter, probably left there by newlywed couples making the traditional visit after their wedding. I strolled along, occasionally meeting others enjoying the warm evening. By now a fingernail moon competed with the bright stars dotting the dark blue sky. Hot dog vendors waited by their carts to accommodate hungry passersby.

I walked under Trinity Bridge, the inclined pedestrian walkway leading into the Kremlin, and I wondered how a country could have called itself atheist for so long with so many significant landmarks bearing names that testified to the reality of God. Then I remembered: atheism was an ideology imposed on the people. They never fully accepted it, and now increasingly rejected it as God revealed Himself through a people free to embrace Him openly without restriction.

As I came out from under Trinity Bridge on the other side, I turned right toward Mokhovia Street. A large lighted billboard stood high over the street in front of me, proclaiming a simple message: *Dorogaya Moya Moakva!* (My Dear Moskva!)

It was time to go. I walked past the sign toward the tunnel entrance to Borovitskaya Metro station. I could hear the music long before I got there. Inside, dressed in their street clothes, their folding chairs forming a circle around well-worn music stands, a string quartet played beautiful Russian melodies. Hurrying commuters stopped to enjoy the elegant sounds magnificently amplified inside the tiled tunnel walls. They probably didn't notice an emotional foreigner standing nearby, bowed in a prayer of thanksgiving.

The Volga River stretched wide and peaceful down below. From the hotel balcony I could see the part of the city that lay across the river, as well as the beautiful rolling countryside beyond. Nizhni Novgorod was indeed a beautiful city, and this was a beautiful Sunday morning. The summer flowers brightened the hillside below and perfumed the air. I was in no hurry for Sasha to pick me up.

As he left me at the hotel the night before he asked, "What will you preach tomorrow?" Before I could answer, he said, "It is Pentecost Sunday, and it is also the first Sunday in the month when we celebrate the Lord's Supper. Perhaps you can combine the two. Oh, and we need to teach our people stewardship. Can you include some words about that?"

As this was his church, I supposed he had a right to be more than an interpreter for the service. But the more he talked, the deeper in the hole I seemed to go. None of the sermons I had prepared would accommodate his requests. God and I had a lot of work to do that night, and for my part I had to stay up much later than I expected. After spending the previous night on the train, I had hoped for a good night's sleep in the hotel. It had been good while it lasted.

After I checked out of the hotel, we left on foot to catch the *tramvai* three blocks away. *Thank You, Lord, for a suitcase with wheels!* After a 20-minute ride, we got off to walk the rest of the way, a full half-mile! *Lord, please let the wheels on my suitcase hold out!*

Arriving a half hour before the service, we waited outside, admiring yet another magnificent church Kentucky Baptists had helped to build. Soon the pastor came and we went in for prayer and instructions for the service. A man who appeared to be a stranger to the group joined us, introducing himself around the room. I would preach second, the pastor told me, between him and Pastor Markhin, Sasha's father-in-law.

Some 300 people crowded into the church as we took our seats on the high platform. We began the service at 10:00, and it was almost noon as time approached for the Lord's Supper. Everyone stood. One of the brothers uncovered an enormous loaf of bread that looked as if it had been baked in a soup kettle. The pastor and the brothers gathered around the table, broke the bread into small pieces, passed it to everyone, and returned to the table. Then they divided the leftovers among the plates and passed them again until all of it was gone.

Next they uncovered the wine—the Russian church uses real wine—serving it from a common cup. Because of the size of this congregation, they used seven cups, passing these among the congregation and returning the remainder to the table this time to stay, unlike the bread.

No one issued an invitation for decision or commitment. No one spoke; there was no music. The pastor and the brothers, their backs to the congregation, began to put things in place on the table and replace the cloths covering the elements. We had been standing since the beginning of the Lord's Supper, through several songs and lengthy Scripture passages as well as the serving of the elements. Still, we stood.

From my vantage point on the platform, I could see the entire congregation. As the brothers and the pastor continued their duties, I saw a middle-aged man move out into the aisle from the back of the church. He made his way forward and nudged one of the brothers, who turned and spoke briefly with him. The brother then spoke with the pastor, who nodded and motioned for the man to kneel where he was. Sasha confirmed what I thought—the man had come to repent.

As the pastor prayed over him, others began to come. Two women about the same age joined the man, also kneeling for prayer. From a section of the balcony reserved for deaf interpretation, a young man came to join them as one of the brothers signed for his communication with the pastor. Then an elderly woman moved into the aisle, knocking her cane off the pew in front of her, also joining the others for prayer.

Five people knelt at the front of the church in repentance, with no invitation and no appeal to come. All over the congregation people wept openly, wiping tears of joy with handkerchiefs and hands. I, too, found my handkerchief.

As the pastor came to the pulpit to conclude the service, the stranger who had appeared in the prayer room before the service came to the front of the church. He asked for permission to speak to the congregation. He wanted to share a testimony.

He had lived in Nizhni Novgorod as a boy. Though his mother had faithfully prayed for him, he never gave his life to Christ. He grew up and moved to a distant city, always mindful that his mother continued to pray for him. Finally he had repented, and he wanted to return to his family home and the church where his mother still attended to share the good news with all of them. With no money for the trip, he had explained his situation to the administrator of the train station in the city where he lived. The administrator allowed him to take the train without paying any fare. As he concluded his testimony, he urged the people never to give up praying for others.

God is doing a marvelous work in Russia, drawing people all over this vast land to Himself. With well over half a century of church repression and official atheism, the Russian people often have no idea how to respond to God's call to faith, but they respond anyway. Russian Baptists are still learning how to reach out to them.

For 5 glorious years, Kentucky Baptists were blessed to walk with them and help them learn and grow. What God did for the Russian Baptists and for us during that time is far more than any one of us will know in this life. But what we do know is that we were part of something far greater than we could ever have envisioned or brought into being. We walked with God!

As I headed back to Moscow, Pastor Alexei Markhin walked with Sasha and me to the train station in Nizhni Novgorod. It had been a marvelous weekend, with a church service I will never forget. During a wonderful afternoon with his family, he and his wife had shared heartbreaking experiences of their life in times such as I would never know. Once again I had found brothers and sisters in Christ who would forever be a part of my life. I searched for words that would not come.

As we reached the station, it was time to say good-bye. "We may never meet again," he said, "but in heaven . . ." He clasped his hands together and looked upward. Knowing that Americans are uncomfortable with the traditional Russian kiss, he graciously offered his hand. I shook it, but it seemed not nearly enough for such a moment.

Interpreters Natasha, Victoria, Elena, Ken and Robbie Murphy, and interpreter Sasha in front of Russian Orthodox Church in Smolensk

Statue of St. George slaying the dragon, Victory Park

The famous Bolshoi Theater in Moscow

Russians enjoying the pools and fountains newly built near the Kremlin, Moscow (above and below)

Cathedral of Christ the Savior (Russian Orthodox), Moscow

Triumphal Arch, Moscow

Afterword

"I'd like to be remembered not for my degrees, for the size of churches I have pastored, not for the great book I hope to write, but that their life is better because our paths have crossed."

Ken Murphy

Ken Murphy's dream was to write a book about the work of Kentucky Baptists in Russia. When Ken began writing this book, he never could have imagined that his life would be cut short before seeing his dream become reality in its final version, but such was the case when Ken was called home to be with the Lord he served so faithfully for many decades. Ken died on July 31, 1999, from complications following surgery. At the time of his death, Ken was the associate director of partnership missions for the Kentucky Baptist Convention.

Ken was never one to call attention to himself, choosing instead that the glory should go to the Lord. Perhaps the above quote from one of Ken's sermons in 1990 best summarizes his life. Ken had been the pastor of several churches in Kentucky, Indiana, Mississippi, and Alabama, but in recent years his passion shifted to missions work with the people of Russia, Poland, and Tanzania as part of Kentucky's partnership missions. It is this passion that is evident in *Russian Harvest.*

Ken was born in Ozark, Alabama, in 1939 and married Robbie Andrews Murphy in 1960. In addition to Robbie, he is survived by two sons and five grandchildren.

It is our sincere hope that this book will serve not as a legacy for Ken Murphy, but as a tribute to the many Christian servants who carry on the Lord's work in Russia and around the world. To God be the glory.

Robbie, Pat, and Greg Murphy

About the author

Ken Murphy was associate director of partnership missions for the Kentucky Baptist Convention. His work with partnership volunteers to Russia, as well as seven trips of his own, provided information and insights for this book. He was a graduate of Samford University and Southern Baptist Theological Seminary (where he earned the master of divinity degree and the doctor of ministry degree) and did additional studies in Russian language at the University of Louisville. He pastored churches in Alabama, Mississippi, Indiana, and Kentucky.